Praise for *In Deep Shift*

"Valerie provides a unique and powerful voice to the new face of spirituality and higher-consciousness living."

Bob Roth
New York Times bestselling author of *Strength in Stillness: The Power of Transcendental Meditation*

"Besides providing illuminating insights and practical suggestions for living in higher consciousness, Valerie Gangas encourages her readers and listeners to seize each opportunity to create a new life, one moment at a time, one choice at a time."

Mirabai Starr
author of *Wild Mercy: Living the Fierce and Tender Wisdom of the Women Mystics*

"Valerie Gangas offers a vision of possibilities of inside-out development. She shows that the core principles of ancient wisdom are practical and usable, even for ambitious, pleasure-loving moderns—all in a style that's funky, witty, engaging, and real. In person, she's all of that and charismatic to boot."

Philip Goldberg
author of *American Veda* and *The Life of Yogananda*

"Valerie Gangas has clearly transcended considerations of personality and entered a bigger mode of being, where her strongest motivating desire is to serve others and make the world better. Val lives a higher truth, and she has managed to convey that in the pages of her new book, *In Deep Shift*."

Jack Forem
New York Times bestselling coauthor of *What the Bleep Do We Know!?*

"With *In Deep Shift*, Valerie Gangas reminds us that even the most devastating and unforeseeable plot twists can help us to grow and evolve. Not only that: with humor and infinite grace, she encourages us to lean into change and even tragedy as a way to strengthen our relationship to meaning, to the Divine, and to life itself."

Ruby Warrington
author of *Sober Curious* and *Women Without Kids*

"*In Deep Shift* is a practical guide for navigating the way forward when facing the challenges of personal awakening. Valerie Gangas offers a fascinating 'from the trenches' perspective that's an invaluable support on the consciousness journey."

Marci Shimoff
#1 *New York Times* bestselling author of *Happy for No Reason* and *Chicken Soup for the Woman's Soul*

in deep shift

Also by Valerie Gangas

Enlightenment Is Sexy

in deep shift

Riding the Waves of
Change to Find Peace,
Fulfillment, and Freedom

Valerie Gangas

sounds true
BOULDER, COLORADO

Sounds True
Boulder, CO 80306

Published 2023

Book design by Meredith Jarrett

Printed in Canada

BK06476

Library of Congress Cataloging-in-Publication Data

Names: Gangas, Valerie, author.
Title: In deep shift : riding the waves of change to find peace,
    fulfillment, and freedom / by Valerie Gangas.
Description: Boulder, CO : Sounds True, 2023.
Identifiers: LCCN 2022035385 (print) | LCCN 2022035386 (ebook) | ISBN
    9781683649656 (hardback) | ISBN 9781683649663 (ebook)
Subjects: LCSH: Change (Psychology) | Attitude (Psychology) |
    Spirituality--Psychology.
Classification: LCC BF637.C4 .G36 2023 (print) | LCC BF637.C4 (ebook) |
    DDC 158.1--dc23/eng/20220914
LC record available at https://lccn.loc.gov/2022035385
LC ebook record available at https://lccn.loc.gov/2022035386

10 9 8 7 6 5 4 3 2 1

Dedicated to my brother, Peter, who taught me that there are no atheists in foxholes, and to my little creature, Frida. I will always love you.

Contents

Introduction

> *"This is who we really are. We are one blink of*
> *an eye away from being fully awake."*
>
> Pema Chödrön

have you ever stepped back, looked at the chaos swirling around you, and thought to yourself, "What the *actual* fuck is happening?" Not just with the specific situation in front of you, but more like, *"What the fuck is happening with my entire existence?!"* If so, there's a real good chance you are *in Deep Shift.*

In deep *what?* What I'm referring to is a profound, core-level shift in consciousness. A radical personal transformation. And I mean *radical.* From soul to skin, inside and outside. Being in Deep Shift *is a sign that a major shift in consciousness is occurring in the deepest levels of your being.* A combo platter of spiritual awakening and paradigm shift, it's the kind of change that makes you say, "Oh my *God*, everything I thought I knew was wrong."

And just like that, boom, you are gifted with a totally new way of seeing, interacting with, and living in the world. You thought you were one way . . . then you "awaken" . . . and you realize you are an entirely different person! This can happen suddenly on the heels of a traumatic life event, or it can happen over time through dedication to a spiritual practice. In some cases, a person may find themself in Deep Shift for no apparent reason at all. The last example is the least common, but however you got here—as you'll come to see in these pages—the good news is that once you accept that you're *in Deep Shift*, anything and everything is possible.

Which might sound a little, shall we say, intense! But honestly? If you have found yourself in this place, then I believe that you have found the meaning of life itself. Having been through the Shift myself and come out the other side reborn, I believe we are all here to wake up, to transform, and to come back home to ourselves, which essentially means coming home to God/the Universe/Source. (I often refer to the "energy" or "creative force" that makes the world spin as *God*, but feel free to use whatever resonates for you. I don't care if you call it Big Bird. In my eyes, it's all the same thing.) A process that essentially means completely letting go of who you thought you were, it's kind of like winning the spiritual lottery. Let me say it loud and clear: being in Deep Shift means you are getting "plugged in." Period. This means you are on your way to living with "higher consciousness" and will find yourself increasingly in tune with the same juju that makes the trees grow and lights up the moon at night.

For example, some commonly reported side effects of being in Deep Shift include: living in the "now," and no longer feeling troubled or distracted by the past or the future; feeling okay to just be you, and no longer feeling daunted, overwhelmed, or discouraged by what others think; having height-ened awareness, and being more consciously connected to your "higher self"; making *waaaay* better decisions, since you're being guided 24/7 by the inner voice that always knows what's best for you; detaching from outcomes (in the healthiest way), so you're not hurt or disappointed by how things turn out; experiencing enhanced mental clarity and creativity, and the ability to absorb information faster and integrate it more deeply; feeling emotionally more grounded and balanced; and regularly getting a good night's sleep.

Sounds pretty cool, doesn't it? And all you have to do to experience the above is . . . give up everything you thought you knew about the person you were, the life you have been living, and all that you believed to be true. Deal?

Don't freak out. From my perspective, being in Deep Shift is the greatest thing that can ever happen to you. Here's how I see it. As the Bhagavad Gita (the most ancient Hindu text and the basis of the yogic philosophy and teachings) states: "The ways of karma are unfathomable. We can never completely know how and why things happen in this world, but we do know that opportunities will show up in all of our lives. Whether we take the leap or not is another story." This means that while not everyone in his or her lifetime will experience the Shift, we are all *built* for transformation. Meaning, we are all born filled with wonder and love, and primed to evolve and to grow throughout the course of our lives. But, over time, the world starts chipping away at our magic. Parents, teachers, religious leaders, politicians, and bosses all—given their own lack of a spiritual hookup—unconsciously lay their power trips on us, steering (or molding) us the way they think is best for us. Which is usually the way that's best for *them*.

Given the way our society is structured, simply being born on this planet means being born into a state of illusion. This illusion leads us to a false sense of identity. Part of our journey therefore is to grow in "knowing" and personal power in order to connect to our true selves, instead of living our lives as the person we've been told we *should* be. This is part of each person's path. It is how we learn and how we grow. And it is the pitfalls and the forks in the road that stretch our awareness and push us to evolve. The good, the bad, and the ugly, it's all there to help us, even when we have zero clue what the hell is happening.

Sadly, our governmental, educational, and social structures have been put in place by people who are, by and large, flying blind. Because despite big expansions of consciousness since the 1960s, at this point in time the scales still haven't tipped. There are more people on the planet who haven't yet "woken up" and experienced the Shift than there are awakened souls. That means that most of society's structures and systems were put in place by humans who have not done the work and crossed the transformation Rubicon. After a while, growing up with this kind of guidance, it's natural for a young person to begin to question their connection to the Divine consciousness that knows everything there is about everything there is. As the pressure begins to build, from friends, family, advertising, and society (it's everywhere!), we slowly start closing down the wonderment in our soul. Our will to go against the grain, to do it "our" way, starts to break down. We get tired. We learn that it's easier to follow the rules (and get super-addicted to all the material "rewards" we get for being compliant). Eventually we are nothing but sheeple, following the leader instead of living to the beat of our own hearts. But more often than not, where they are going is a long, dry, and dusty road leading to nowhere truly fulfilling.

And then one day something curious happens: a crack appears in the facade. Maybe it comes after years of managing the anxiety of living the way I described earlier with a regular yoga or meditation practice, or perhaps it shows up in the midst of a particularly challenging life experience. But, as if we've found a secret doorway to a whole other Universe, it is through this crack that we get a teeny glimpse of who we *really* are. A child of the Cosmos. Effortlessly connected to everything that is and flowing like a wave on the Ocean of Life.

With this comes the realization that the way you have been living is *all wrong!* Now that you've seen "the light," nothing about your life makes sense, as if you've been operating on a wonky frequency this whole time and now you've tuned in to a signal that's speaking directly to your soul. Surveying the landscape of what *used* to be your life, you look back and begin to connect the dots. You're able to see how everything you've experienced during your lifetime has, in fact, been leading you to this point—but that now you're here, the "old" way of doing things will no longer cut it. You have moved on from the level of logic and reason and into the realm of feeling, intuition, and living from the seat of your soul. You are officially *in Deep Shift* . . . which is where the real fun begins.

Because *now* comes the time for you to truly carve your own path. After all, it is increasingly obvious that being a mature, switched on, fully functioning adult human is NOT about getting a degree, clocking into a stable job, and living in the suburbs with 2.5 children and a brand-new Lexus. It is about breaking free from the rules of the earthly road and deeply connecting with the power that makes the planet spin. This is true power. Personal, universal, cosmic power. Which means the time has come to un-brainwash yourself from everything you have been told about who you are and what the fuck life is all about and begin writing your own rules for living.

Which is also where this book comes in. Navigating your way through this new terrain often proves to be no easy task, my friend. Great forces will try to pull you back into your old ways of thinking and doing. People won't want to see you change. Society won't want to make space for you to expand. You being in Deep Shift will put others on edge, and managing *their* discomfort can be the most challenging part of all. Which means you're gonna have to stand up for what you know is true and learn to depend on yourself as you walk bravely into your new life. And when you can't see the enchanted forest for the trees, I'll be dropping bread crumbs throughout these pages to help you find your way.

So, who the hell am I for you to be entrusting me with nothing short of your real-time rebirth into a whole new paradigm? Let me begin by saying that by no stretch of the imagination do I have ALL the answers. Nobody does. But I have found myself being dragged through the Shift on many an occasion. Navigating my own awakening, I have also taken a deep dive into the world of expanded consciousness, and, yes, I have a lot to say on the subject.

It began at the beginning for me, as I was born a highly sensitive person. I didn't have a name for it then, but from an early age I was tapped into the emotional and spiritual energy of my environment. Does this resonate with you? I was also highly intuitive. I could size a person up in one minute flat, as if I could literally "see" into them. I also grew up with a very sensitive and intuitive mother (in another era she might legit have been branded a witch), and I'm convinced she passed on that good juju to yours truly.

When I was nine years old, my mom took me to meet Mother Teresa in a little Catholic church in the Pilsen area of Chicago, where I grew up. At the time, I had no idea who this saintly woman was. I just knew I was going on an adventure with my mom. When we got to the church, we sat down in one of the pews, and when I turned around to look, I saw about forty women dressed in blue-and-white saris. *Wow,* I found myself wondering, *who are these beautiful women, and why are they so shiny?*

After Mass, we all got a chance to meet Mother Teresa. I walked up to her, and when she took my hand, looking deeply into my eyes, something shifted inside of me, as if a light was turned on in my soul that never went out. In a haze, I asked my mom, *"Who is that lady?"* My mom smiled and calmly told me, *"That lady* single-handedly changed the world, my love."

My obsession with all things spiritual and mystical was confirmed right then and there. By junior high I was devouring books by both the Christian mystics and modern spiritual teachers like Louise Hay and Wayne Dyer. My mom, being a former nun and a mystical poet, was right there by my side to answer all my questions. I wasn't the best student at school, and I can remember my magical mother saying to me, "Val, just do what you need to do to pass your classes and come home and read whatever you want." Mom was awake, so she knew the system was bogus. By encouraging my mystical studies, I can now see that she was both protecting me from falling into the trap of living somebody else's life and empowering me to have the strength to be my own person.

I went on to major in comparative religious studies in college and then got my master's degree in transpersonal psychology. As I said, I've been endlessly curious about spirituality, and what *really* makes us tick, for as long as I can remember. And that's another trait of mine that I bet you see in yourself, too, as many of those who find ourselves in Deep Shift have been fascinated with spirituality and mysticism from an early age.

As you can tell, my relationship with my mom was super-special, and it was when she passed away due to breast cancer in 2011 that I first found myself in Deep Shift. My world fell apart completely. I thought I would never meet another person who understood me the way she did, and, in the weeks after she passed, I became suicidal. My entire world went black, and I sunk to the depths of despair. I felt as though I had lost EVERYTHING . . . and, in a way, I had. I had no idea who I *was* without my mom. It was as though my entire identity had been shattered, and now, like Humpty Dumpty, I had to put myself back together. What I didn't realize, even after years of studying theology, miracles, and spirituality, is that *this is what transformation looks like*. But nothing, and I mean nothing, could have prepared me for what came next.

A couple of months after losing my mom, I had hit my limit. I found myself on the floor of my shower, on my hands and knees, begging God to either save me or help me take my life. I couldn't go on anymore; the pain was just too much. It also felt as though the person I was had *already* died, and as if there was nothing left to keep me in this life.

About a week later, an ex-boyfriend who was extremely worried about me insisted I come to his company's business dinner just to get me out of the house. I happened to be seated next to a random man who I struck up a conversation with. In about two minutes flat I was bawling my eyes out, telling him that I was suicidal. Clearly, I was in a really bad space. He was very kind to me and suggested I learn how to meditate. Specifically, he nudged me to learn Transcendental Meditation.

For some reason, I decided to take this stranger's advice, and within a couple weeks I found myself at a meditation center on Lake Shore Drive in Chicago. Part of me likes to believe that my mom was helping me from the other side and that she nudged, or rather shoved, me toward meditation. Transcendental Meditation (TM for short) is a mantra-based meditation. You learn with a trained teacher who gives you a mantra (a sound you repeat in your head while meditating) in a special little ceremony with flowers and deities, and next thing you know, you're off to the races.

In my case, the TM teacher and I both closed our eyes, I began to think the mantra to myself . . . and just like that, *I was gone*. I dove into a part of my body and mind I never knew existed—a space that felt boundless, limitless, and totally awesome. It felt like I fell into an ocean of silence inside my own body. As if I had opened the door to heaven, except it was inside of me. When I opened my eyes twenty minutes later, I knew I had experienced something profound. In that moment, I was transformed. Everything was different. Colors looked brighter, sounds were clearer, the air smelled sweet, and I felt as if all the darkness inside of me had completely lifted. As if I was seeing the world through God's eyes, everything around me was holy and perfect. Never again would I be the same person, and soon I would discover that I had only glimpsed the tip of the iceberg.

It took me a couple of weeks to adjust to this new feeling, but *man*, it was incredible. I would feel completely fulfilled just looking at trees and being outside with the birds. I felt as if I was connected to ALL of it. As if I *was* the grass, I *was* the little squirrel running around in the yard, I *was* the homeless person on the corner. I was the Universe—and I knew it. And I hadn't even dropped any acid! My fourteen-year sleeping problem also disappeared, literally overnight. Looking back, my experience of learning TM was nothing short of miraculous—and I will be forever grateful to the man who suggested I try it.

After all, the real mindblower was that only a few weeks previously I had been planning to give away my dog, along with all my belongings, and *end my life*. Without my mom, I could not see how I could go on living. I'd sobbed and wailed myself to sleep, night after night, desperately praying for a balm for my grief and an end to the shitty sadness in my soul. I *never* could have guessed it would come in the form of something as simple as *meditation*.

But when I say this was the tip of the iceberg, I mean that things only continued to get more interesting. Once I repaid my sleep debt, my mind was clear as a bell. Not that I even really had to think—I could just follow the signs. Synchronicity was everywhere, and it would simply be obvious what I should do next. My destiny was being laid out before me, and I just kept walking into it.

I also began having visions, and I discovered I had the ability to communicate with people who had passed away. The day after I learned TM, I had an unclouded vision of my mom with Christ. In one second, all the terror I had experienced after she died was dissolved. I knew where she was; in fact, in that moment I felt like I completely understood death. And so, the fear of dying also went right out the window. I remember telling my meditation teacher two very profound things. The first thing I said to her when I opened my eyes was, "Everything I thought I knew was wrong." Days later, I explained that I felt as though all humans had the ability to know *anything*. Not like all of a sudden I was going to be a chemist; more as if a deep spiritual knowledge was baked into all of our cells. The *Deep Shift* that I had experienced was allowing me to tap into this cosmic information. I just knew things; I didn't have to ask why or how. I just knew. Like Dorothy in *The Wizard of Oz*, I realized I had always had the power—I'd just never fully realized it.

So that's my story. What's yours? We all have a different path, and you can find yourself in Deep Shift without reaching the kind of rock bottom I did. I clearly needed a big bop on the head to wake up, but I was always a stubborn little bugger. Whatever it is that brought you here, what's actually happening is that you are ready to start living the life that's really *yours* to live. Given how challenging it can be to wade through Deep Shift, a friend or fellow traveler on the spiritual highway is an invaluable source of support on this glorious—and yet sometimes stinky—path. And while the people around you might not understand what's happening, I certainly do. So, it's very good we found each other, as things can get hairy.

For example, you may find yourself unexpectedly moving, switching careers, or leaving an old relationship. Perhaps you get involved with a new group of people, and gossiping and shallow chit-chat (if it's something you have engaged with) may start to feel icky or mind-numbingly boring to you. You may feel called to "bump up" your spiritual practice, and it's quite possible you will want to spend more time in nature. If you've been super-attached to a certain career path, this may come into question too, as you no longer see the point in working simply to make money. Hidden talents, interests, and passions can pop up, and, in a heartbeat, move you in a new direction. Supernatural abilities may also arise (sounds weird, yep, but discovering you are "psychic" can be pretty darn cool!).

Meanwhile, your nervous system is naturally becoming more sensitive, meaning it may feel like your whole personality is changing, as if you are seeing the world with completely new eyes. This part might be especially confusing, as if you have a *whole new brain*. Which, of course, means you will have to relearn how to use it! This will mainly mean developing the capacity to trust in all your own decisions, and no longer asking for permission or validation about how to do *you*. You are officially taking the road less traveled, and you're the one drawing the map! You can aid this process by paying extra attention to the food you eat, how much you drink, and generally fine-tuning your caregiving of your entire physical vehicle (your brain, your body, *and* your emotions).

The good news? I—as in this book—got you, boo! In these pages, I will be guiding you through each step of the process of being in Deep Shift, and sharing simple, clear-cut action steps that will help you navigate your way forward. The process of awakening can be defined in the simplest terms as a dropping of what's "false" in order to embrace what is "real" . . .

and each chapter of this book contains a beefy tool kit of action steps and paradigm-shifting ideas to make the transition as easy as possible.

I've divided the text into three parts, reflecting the different stages of a classic Deep Shift. This begins with acknowledging WTF is happening, and that from here on, this will never be the same again. As such, part 1 is designed to help you orient yourself on the Shifter path. From there, it's about gathering the tools to help you handle what's coming atcha with as much grace (and as little anxiety) as humanly possible. To this end, part 2 will walk you through my tried-and-true tools for staying grounded and sticking the landing. And finally, anybody who has experienced Deep Shift will essentially have to relearn how to be in a world that's been turned upside down and inside out. Part 3 goes deep (naturally) into how to navigate this transition and reap all the amazing benefits of making it through and out the other side.

Ultimately, I want to guide you to a place where you no longer feel the need to compromise yourself for image, attention, safety, money, or status. To a place where you begin to find more clarity and inner strength, as your attention naturally attunes with what brings you greater joy and fulfillment. As you read along, my hope is that you will find yourself living with more faith and less fear, a shift that will be reflected in both your day-to-day choices and your "major" life decisions. Woohoo, now you're cooking with gas! You will start feeling a sense of magic and unexpected grace creeping into all areas of your life. And all of sudden, you wake up one day and realize it's actually no longer possible for you to live an "ordinary" life. Trust me, when I found myself in Deep Shift, even going to the grocery store became an awe-inspiring experience. And what I quickly realized is that my sense of wonder had always been there—I just couldn't see or feel it.

Growing up in a Greek household, I had been fed a lot of set ideas about how things should be. You grow up, get married, get a house near your parents, and raise a family. On the inside, these "rules" never felt like they fit me—and as soon as the lights went on (i.e., the Shift started hitting the fan), the rulebook went right out the window. For the first time, I felt like I was living a life on my own terms. No religious dogma, no societal programming, and no family dynamic was going to pull me back in. I just *knew*—and continue to know—what was right for *me,* and that was that.

Do you know how kick-ass it feels to live like this? No more wondering, no more stressing over the small stuff. No. You are here, you are clear, and you are ready to live *your* life. And the coolest part? Since you now know exactly who you are and what you actually want and need, the Universe can get 100 percent behind you, too. You can feel the cosmic wind in your sails, guiding you toward the deepest desires that reside in your heart of hearts.

Which all sounds pretty incredible, right? And it *is*; just don't expect it to come easily. Once you're in Deep Shift, the best piece of advice I can give you is not to give up. To keep going. To keep learning and growing. I will walk side by side with you and do my best to pick you up when you fall.

Now that you know why you're here and what goodies lie in store, let's chat about the fact that you are *so* not alone as you find yourself wading through the Shift. There are lots of people, just like us, experiencing exactly what you're going through. In fact, there are so many of us on the planet right now, I've given us a name: Shifters. Although we come from all walks of life, Shifters share certain traits, such as being highly sensitive, deeply intuitive, and capable of profound states of awareness. We also have a natural interest in spirituality and the unseen world. Why? It's our sensitivity. The very same "gift" that can make the world seem so cruel and abrasive sometimes is also what connects us to a higher power.

No doubt some of this resonates with you. You may have felt this way your whole life but repressed it as you tried to fit in and go along with society's plans for you. Well, let me share a little theory I have about that. I believe that we Shifters are here to help the rest of society open up to the next level of consciousness, too, and to do it with the utmost compassion, love, and understanding. While everyone else is on the hamster wheel of life, we're tapping into the unseen world to bring back information that will push the spiritual envelope. And what's more, when we're aware of this role and actually living it, we have the ability to transform people simply by being us. This connection to a higher power also makes us way more powerful than we know. You, my friend, are a force of nature.

In my work as a transformational coach and spiritual guide, I've come across tons of people who are in Deep Shift as well as many who have made great strides in their spiritual lives. In addition to being more tapped into the world than the average person, their intuition is off the charts, while their heightened sensitivity to the cosmic energies helps them navigate this world in a very magical way. I've also observed that many of these people had a traumatic childhood or have experienced some extreme challenges in their lives—a connection that makes complete sense to me.

Any time a person experiences a traumatic life event, it is as if the ground has been pulled out from underneath their feet. Whatever you took for granted about the safety of the world—that your parents would be there to protect you, that your body would function just fine, or that you'd have a job to pay the bills, for example—no longer stands. As such, you now have no option but to rely on your *intuitive knowing* as a way to navigate your life. You must remain on high alert for alarm bells going off in order to protect yourself. For better or for worse, this heightens your sensitivity to the world around you and strengthens your intuitive muscle.

And speaking of the ground being pulled out from underneath our feet . . . I wrote this introduction during the COVID-19 pandemic. I'd never lived through a global crisis like this, but a lot of my older friends who experienced the Vietnam War and the social uprisings of the 1960s and 1970s have told me that the pandemic has had a similar flavor. Having already got a taste of a *global* shift in consciousness, they're like, *"Here we go again!"* Which adds a whole other layer to the concept of being in Deep Shift.

With the entire *world* transforming, the energy is INTENSE out there to say the least. The cosmic pot is being stirred up, forcing the kind of big life reckonings that are landing people in Deep Shift en masse. Cue mass confusion and uncertainty about who we are and where we're going as a society; and so this book will also help you sort through the confusion of the external world and stay on the path to personal freedom.

As much as I can't tell you the specifics of how this is all gonna play out, I can make you at least one solid promise: I will always be honest with you. Because the truth is, transformation ain't all unicorns and rainbows. The Shift is about to hit the fan, and you will encounter many obstacles along the way. The most important thing is to confront each one head on and lay it all out on the table. Know that whatever roadblocks show up along the way, I see it as my job to help you be as prepared as humanly possible for them.

To this day, I think about what my mom told me about Mother Teresa and ask myself, *How can just* one person *change the goddamned world?* The answer I arrive at is always the same: it's not about one person amassing the power or influence to change the world, which is the way most people think about it. The thing is, when you change, everything changes. This means that just one individual stepping into their individual power fully and authentically makes a dent in the way the world operates. Which is the real reason anybody finds themselves in Deep Shift, and the real reason why you're here.

part one

Okay, WTF is Going On?

CHAPTER 1

You Are Not Losing It, You Are in Deep Shift

"We don't see things as they are;
we see them as we are."

Anaïs Nin

et me guess. Things are changing for you in a major way. I'm going to go out on a limb and say you're probably questioning everything, and that, very possibly, it feels like you are actually losing your shit. It may be difficult to put into words exactly what you're feeling, but what you're experiencing is very . . . different. Kind of like you're an alien who woke up on the wrong planet. I get it, trust me.

So, first of all, why is this happening? Why, all of a sudden, does it feel like you are living in an alternate universe? Let's talk it out.

Basically, your number is up. Your time has come. The boom has been lowered. You are officially *in Deep Shift* and there is no going back. Let's check your vitals. Do you feel like you are going totally crazy? Check. Are you questioning everything you thought you knew? Check. Are you ready to jump out of your skin, dump your old life, and make some big-ass changes? Check, check, and check. We have a winner! But first it's going to feel like a fucking hurricane came blowing through your reality. Hang on to your hat my friend, shit is about to get realz.

Now, I appreciate that what I've told you about my Deep Shift makes it sound pretty darned far out. Not everybody reading this will literally find themselves having visions and speaking to dead people. But whatever your unique set of circumstances, entering Deep Shift will likely lead to a profound shift in your worldview. Perhaps you're having ideas about quitting your job and walking the Camino de Santiago in Spain. Selling all of your possessions and living a very simple, borderline monk-like existence. Ditching ALL of your old friends and starting over. Or maybe you've just had someone close to you pass away, especially if it happened abruptly, tragically, with a lot of heartache involved or out of the blue, and the loss has turned your whole worldview on its head. Whatever it is, if you have to go to one more cocktail party and talk about nothing, you are seriously going to go fucking postal. Looking at the way you have been living, you are likely thinking to yourself, ummmm, that's not gonna work for me anymore. When can I get the first plane out of Dodge?

On the plus side, you don't know why, but it's also like you just *know* things now. In fact, you're pretty sure the Universe is reading your mind because, holy cow, is the synchronicity flowing! You start thinking about a new career, and out of the blue, you meet somebody who's an expert in the exact field you were dreaming about. When this was happening to me (oh yeah, I've been there), I found I had a strong desire to move to the countryside. I even had a vision of myself living in a brown cedar house, located down a long driveway. Why? I had no idea! I had been living in the middle of Chicago for twenty years, but that cedar house kept showing up. I would see it in my dreams or find myself visualizing it as I went about my day.

Wouldn't you know it, within weeks I found myself in Iowa (a totally spontaneous trip; I decided that morning to drive there) signing a year-long lease on . . . guess what? You got it, a cedar house in the middle of the country with the longest driveway you ever did see. And well, experiences like this are about to become your norm. But when they first start happening, it can be a total mind fuck. There's going to be a lot of, WHAT THE HELL WAS THAT? going on. Not that you know how to work the controls yet, but you are now operating on an entirely different frequency. Welcome to Opposite Land: as in, this is the opposite of how life used to go for you.

As for the part about feeling like you're losing your shit? In a way, you are, as your old ways of doing and seeing things begin to fly out the window. *Of course* this feels confusing. *It makes sense* that this would throw you off your game for a while. But it's going to be okay. In fact, you are about to go on the ride of your life. There is going to be some serious bucking going on, but just hold on. The chips are about to fall majorly in your favor.

But before we go there, you may be asking (in the words of the great David Byrne): *"Well, how did I get here?"*

As I discussed in the introduction, it's likely you arrived at this point on the heels of a major life event. *What do I mean by "major life event"?* In this chapter, I'd like to focus in on what I consider to be the top five kinds of experiences that precede people finding themselves in Deep Shift. But before I begin, let's be real: some of these paths can be painful and downright traumatic. Pain *itself* may be responsible for bringing on a case of Deep Shift. But each of the five life-changing experiences I'll be describing in this chapter can *also* be doorways to radical transformation. And with a true-blue heightened consciousness, you'll likely look back and see this or that pathway—no matter how temporarily intense it got—as a sacred gift. There are no mistakes in this world, people. The Universe/God knows what the heck it's doing.

One more bit about the latent power in pain—whether physical, psychological, or emotional. The thing is, we humans don't like pain. Or any kind of discomfort, for that matter. We will do whatever it takes to avoid it. But like the old saying goes, "You can run, but you can't hide." What I mean is, I believe we are on this planet to expand. To leave the earth a little wiser than when we first made our grand entrance. This means there are cosmic systems in place to shake up our lives and nudge us, sometimes with a cattle prod, to move forward and make the necessary life choices in order to grow. If we stay stagnant, the discomfort of staying stuck in a life we have outgrown becomes a dull pain that can't be cured by an Advil or a bong hit. Transformation is necessary to become the person you were meant to be: that is, a bad-ass, self-actualized human being. And when it comes to being pushed into making ground-floor, consciousness-altering shifts, guess how it usually happens? Ding, ding, ding! SO often the correct answer is through PAIN. Yikes!

This is because it's only when we've been brought to our knees (by whatever or whoever) that we stop pretending we're in control and that we have all the answers: that is, we reach a place of surrender. Humans are stubborn, and often this can only occur when we've been so beat down and humbled that we've given up. This is when the Universe/God/Higher Power/Great Spirit gets to swoop in, pick our sorry asses up, and give us a fresh, new perspective and way of doing this thing called life. And thus begins the next chapter.

But before we get there, we must enter into Deep Shift. The renowned Trappist monk, mystic, and social activist Thomas Merton referred to this period of darkness before the dawn as "the dark night of the soul," a time when you are asked to face "the False Self and the True Self." Father Richard Rohr, a best-selling spiritual author and Franciscan friar, talks about it as being the crossroads of "the first and second half of life," though this could happen at any age. And while the Big Kahuna Deep Shift typically happens only once in a person's life, some people may have numerous "Shift-like episodes" occur—which usually come on the heels of the Big One. Kinda like aftershocks. The fact is, once you step onto this path you will forever be evolving. Until the day you die. For some people, that major Shift may only come in the moments before their last breath. But this is something we would like to avoid. Wake up when you are young, why don't you, so you actually get to experience all the magic in the world!

If this is sounding daunting, remember what C. S. Lewis once said: "Hardships often prepare ordinary people for an extraordinary destiny." It's when we're able to stand strong and consciously walk forward through our own "dark night of the soul" that we also come to learn that pain is our friend on the road to transformation. It's the one thing that gets us to really "See" with a capital *S*. This is because pain is often the result of a shattering of delusion, and of being confronted with the way things really are (versus how we would like them to be). Seeing the world with this level of clarity requires an inner strength—cuz it ain't all roses out there! Pain cuts through the BS and brings TRUTH to the way we perceive the world around us. Being able to see what's really going on gives us what I call a "spiritual edge" and delivers us back to our power: living a life of integrity, love, and inner riches.

You are a change-maker and a force to be reckoned with. You are your own person, and in a world of ego BS and false belief systems, this gives you an advantage, for to know thyself is the path to ultimate freedom. Hallelujah. Can I get an AMEN?!

And so, onward we go.

The Five Pathways to Deep Shift

As for how we find ourselves in Deep Shift, there are as many versions of events as there are human beings. But in my experience, the following five are some surefire ways to get there.

Grief and Deep Shift

In September 2018 my brother passed away from acute lymphoblastic leukemia. He was forty-six years old and my only sibling. My blood. One of my rocks. In fact, in the past eight years I have lost nine of my close family members, including my mom and brother. This being so, I have learned a great deal about grief and transformation through losing so many people I've deeply loved. The one sure thing I can tell you about grief is that it has a life all its own. In the aftermath of a loss, grief holds the reins. Grief is in charge.

When someone you love passes, first there's a period of shock. *Then* comes the pain: core-level, gut-wrenching pain pulling you into a darkness like you have never known, where you begin to doubt you will ever experience lightness and laughter again—as if someone has shut the curtains on your life. And we know by now what often comes on the heels of this sort of pain. Yep! *Welcome to Deep Shift.*

In the wake of any kind of loss, be it the loss of a person you love, or the loss of a marriage, a career, or even an experience where you experience a loss of self, you have two choices. You can either use this shocking heartbreak to find out more about who you *really* are and what's important to you, and then use this newfound self-awareness to sign a new lease on life, or you can turn into that person who closes down and just numbs out to avoid the pain. The problem with option B? Turning your back on prompts to look inward after a deep dive into the grief pool will only signal to the Universe that that kick in the nuts didn't do the trick. That you're going to need some *more* shitty experiences to help you get with the program. With a caveat: it's okay to acknowledge that you may not be ready for a Deep Shift at this point in time and that you need some time and space to recover before stepping off the shore and sailing into a New World.

In my case, I had no choice but to turn my pain into power. To choose alchemy. For me, writing about my personal experiences of grief and transformation was what turned my life around and led me to connect with others on this path.

Grief is something we all experience at some point during our lives, and in many ways it helps us begin to understand and become less afraid of death and other kinds of endings. We unmask the mechanics of how we die, we get to contemplate up-close and personal the question of where we "go," and we learn how to deal with being left behind. For example, when my brother passed away, I was the only one who stayed by his side. Everyone else had backed away because the situation was just too intense. We had to take him off life support, so the energy in the room was really heavy. I made a conscious decision, in that moment, that if I couldn't help my brother live, I was going to help him die. I also had my medium and her team helping him cross over to the other side. I had one hand on his head and one on his chest, and I kept beaming my thoughts into him: "You can do this. You are safe. Everyone is going to be waiting for you (since most of our family is dead). I love you." When he died, I felt his energy come right through my body. In that second, I knew he was okay, I knew where he was going, and, in a way, I also knew what it felt like to die. It was extraordinary and a gift from God.

Grief may lead you into therapy, or instigate a move, a career change, or a divorce. All of these experiences can kick-start a period of Deep Shift. I promise you: losing someone you really love will alter you forever. The question is, which way do you want to go from here?

When it happened to me, I focused on the positive lessons and holy experiences that are naturally birthed from that level of grief, as it was the only way to save myself. I realized how strong I was. How connected to God I was. I discovered my ability to truly surrender. To give it ALL up to a higher power because I could no longer carry the burden alone. In short, grief broke me open and allowed the magic to flow in. I'm also reminded of something my mom liked to say: "The bad doesn't stay bad forever." Now, I have something of my own to add to this: the "bad" always happens for a reason, which is often to lead you to the "good." We humans always seem to need some sort of a shove in order to wake up. What I discovered is that when we go deep into our grief we learn the power of a heart that has been broken . . . *open*. A discovery that leads us right into the arms of Deep Shift.

Illness and Deep Shift

Facing sickness, whether it's ourselves who are sick or somebody close to us, helps a person gain some serious clarity about why you're on this planet and what your life is about. And at light speed. No longer being able to rely on our physical body makes us take a hard look at our lives and reevaluate how we want to live moving forward—something many of us have experienced during COVID, with people leaving their jobs and making other major changes in mass numbers. Let alone all that time spent in a corporate role you can't stand, perhaps facing sickness also made you realize that all the years spent *worrying* about everything was just a total waste. When going into battle with an illness that is dead-set on ravaging your physical being, looking dumb at a networking event suddenly doesn't seem like that big of a deal. It's perspective time.

Meanwhile, anyone who has taken care of a sick family member or friend knows how this selfless act can also be transformational. In helping another in need, we are given the opportunity to face our own greatest fears, as well as get a new perspective on how we see ourselves. Taking care of sick friends and family members has reminded me that when the chips are down, the only things that matter are love and God—and that you might as well live as if this is the case now! The earlier you can get this memo, the freer your life will be. Powerful stuff, and another portal to Deep Shift.

Until sickness comes knocking, we tend to skip along Easy Street, taking the well-traveled path and ignoring the ever-present reality that *nothing* in this physical world is a given. It usually takes a "Grade A episode" (like what I experienced with my brother at the end of his battle with leukemia) to catapult us into appreciating the raw reality of how temporal, precious, and sacred life actually is. How much responsibility comes with having a physical body. How much life *matters*. How much *our loved ones* matter. How much *we* matter.

After a serious car wreck, a terrible health scare, or a grave illness (again, either our own or that of someone we love), Deep Shift is often just around the corner—as we are often asked to align with "something greater than ourselves." Meaning, literally, something way bigger than our body and more far out than anything we can imagine with our minds. When you realize that you are a soul living in a sack of meat, you can't help but start to expand.

For many people, when illness comes knocking and they are confronted by the limitations of the physical body, they find themselves subconsciously picking a number and getting in line for the doorway to Deep Shift—with amazing results. I've known people who were told by their doctors that they only had months to live . . . and then they turned around and did more in those few months than they had in their entire adult lives! But only as a result of accepting the real possibility they weren't going to make it. In short, having your mortality shoved in your face is a surefire way to get your ass in gear.

Still, the "time" component can play into this, too. One person may find themselves on the path to awakening right at the outset of discovering they have a life-altering illness or receiving some other Shift-worthy news. But others may require more time to process, reflect, reevaluate, and release—or to simply catch up emotionally with what's going down—before the light bulb comes on and their Deep Shift comes into view.

Recovery and Deep Shift

Many people find themselves in Deep Shift after hitting rock bottom and getting sober from addiction—more common than you might think. One in ten Americans are thought to have resolved a serious substance use problem, and that's not taking into account addictions to things like food, sex, and work, or all the "gray area" users who have also found it in them to quit. Choosing to be fully present to life, without numbing out with your substance (or behavior) of choice, can bring on the Deep Shift vibes. When you've spent half your life in a numbed-out stupor, sobriety *is* the altered state.

Not to mention that the twelve-step program for recovery is one of the most profound paths to transformation out there. Don't think this applies to you? The chief aim of these programs is to help individuals tap into and align themselves with a "power greater than yourself"—what the programs term "a God of your own understanding" (yup, Big Bird)—in order to become free from obsessive-compulsive enslavement or addiction/attachments. In other words, to live in a more "awakened" and present state! I have personal experience of this. In my case, it wasn't a terrible addiction to one thing in particular, it was a *little too much* of many things. I felt like maybe I ate a little too much, drank a little too much, and spent a little too much money. Being an all-or-nothing kind of a gal, I was looking for balance in these areas. Knowing a few people in my circle who were or are using twelve-step programs to work through their addictions made me curious about this particular approach to healing and transformation. What I found was one of the most deeply spiritual and life-affirming programs I've ever come across. Like, the kind of inner healing and acceptance people get from years—decades!—of therapy. And it's free!

Even though my overeating hadn't brought me to my knees, I wanted to know exactly what these programs do for people. So, I attended AA (Alcoholics Anonymous), NA (Narcotics Anonymous), DA (Debtors Anonymous), and OA (Overeaters Anonymous) meetings for six months. I also partnered with an OA sponsor so I could "work the steps." I felt a strong desire to experience, firsthand, exactly how transformation can occur through this specific spiritual program. And what I found is a legit gateway to living a kick-ass, awakened life.

If the goal is to get to the truth of who we are and how we want to live, a twelve-step program can get you there. As well as connecting you in a very real way to the concept of a Higher Power, the focus is on radical honesty with yourself and others. This honesty chips away at the years of BS that most of us have built our lives around, and eventually you find your true self: that is, a child of the Universe. Essentially, it feels like what church *should be.* A group of people who are coming together simply to help each other. A space where people can be vulnerable and honest without the fear of judgment. A place to heal, to connect with others, and to connect with each person's own Higher Power. Somewhere along the way, right around when the humans who decided they were in charge took it upon themselves to do the work of the universal Higher Power, our churches and religious institutions forgot that it can be this simple.

I was hands-down a different person after going through all twelve steps with my sponsor—to the point that I now believe the program should be taught everywhere, from schools to open-to-the-public seminars and every other possible avenue in between. And to top it off—I'll say it again—it is FREE! I'm also speaking to everyone here. Twelve-step programs are available in most US cities, and while being grounded in the practicality of daily life, they are also incredibly holy (but NOT in a creepy, God-bothering way). And did I mention they're free?

Miracles and Deep Shift

Perhaps because of the sheer volume of shitty life experiences I've been through, I am a card-carrying member of the miracles club. I truly believe that miracles happen *every damned day*. A miracle can be a medical breakthrough, the love of your life sitting down next to you in a diner, or you just experiencing a moment of knowing that you are connected to everything and everyone. Miracles are for realz, people; you don't even have to believe in them. And just like the "bad" experiences noted earlier, the "good" ones can equally guide a person into Deep Shift.

I love the quote "With God, all things are possible" (Matthew 19:26). Because the truth is, life can change in an instant. It certainly happened to me, so I know how the story goes. One minute you're walking along, living life as you know it, and BAM! Grace falls strongly upon you and suddenly you're a different person. I have described this experience as seeing the world with totally new eyes. God's eyes. My definition of a "miracle" is when something happens that goes against everything you believed was possible and "proves" that the world is a magical place. When you experience a miracle, it blows your mind. You can't believe that this could happen! To you, of all people! It makes you grateful and humble, as if you were being shown great mercy for no other reason except that the Universe loves you.

Learning to meditate was my "miracle," the thing that saved me after I became suicidal following the loss of my mom. After I learned to meditate, the whole world looked different to me. It was like I landed on a different planet. I walked in the door thinking about how I was going to end my life and I left feeling like the world was the most incredible place I had ever seen. The level of peace in my soul was otherworldly, and there was so much love in my heart that I thought it was going to explode. As I already shared, the very first thing I remember saying after my first session was, "Everything I thought I knew was wrong"—which has become something of a personal catchphrase. Why do I love it so much? This sentiment gets to the very core and heartbeat of the nature of Deep Shift. When our perception shifts in such a fundamental, overnight way, we immediately realize our old life is now as dead as a doornail and there is simply no going back, as if we're working with an entirely new set of rules.

When the "impossible" happens, extraordinary changes can immediately begin to occur in our lives—simply because you are no longer limited by what you believe *is* possible. And what follows from there? That's right, you're in Deep Shift! A miracle in our lives can set in motion profound changes in every aspect of reality. The supernatural kicks in and takes over. It's unexpected, sure . . . and unbelievable, of course . . . but this route to Deep Shift can facilitate the ultimate activation of a person's divine potential.

Meditation and Deep Shift

Let me be clear: when I talk about meditation, I'm not just talking about sitting cross-legged with your eyes closed. I'm talking about approaching meditation as a practice that has the potential to transform one's interior life and one's entire consciousness, from the ground up. To unravel the blockages and dip beyond the obsessions, distractions, ego-driven stories, and monkey mind to establish a spiritual edge: in this case, an increasingly strong conscious connection with the Divine within.

As much as it was my mom's death that set me on the pathway to Deep Shift, my personal story of becoming a full-blown Shifter was born out of meditation. It led me to an inner awakening, forever altering my conscious awareness. I had finally found the tool that could take me on a much-needed inward journey. Once you open the door to your soul, all sorts of goodies come out. In my case, it blew the door right off the hinges, catapulting me further into Deep Shift! And even though my experience may seem unique, I know from having shared it while speaking to groups all over the country for two-plus years that people of all ages and from all walks of life can relate to and identify with meditation as being the gateway to an expanded level of consciousness and way of seeing and being in the world.

For me, meditation is a simple-to-open doorway to limitless and boundless dimensions of life, which exists within all people. I took such a deep dive inward that it unlocked something inside of me. It was like I entered into a world inside of me that I never knew existed. By practicing regularly, we can all cultivate an awareness of our boundlessness and nurture an increasingly abiding awareness of our "true self," a fundamental part of the process of Deep Shift.

So, there you have my top five gateways to Deep Shift. Of course, there are many other life-changing events that can send us on the path. You could get divorced, lose your job, take a deep dive into yoga, fast for an extended period of time, have a near-death experience, or fall in love. All of these very human experiences can lead to a major shift in consciousness, a new life path, and an entire new way of being. But what these examples have in common is that sensitivity, pain, otherworldly experiences, and periods of serious questioning work together on a person. Until, yes, anybody who has experienced one or more of these transformational paths can confidently say that at one point or another, we thought we were completely losing our shit. It's par for the course. And, honestly, it's the whole point.

How can you expect to move forward into unchartered territories of consciousness without losing your grip on what came before? If anything, "losing it" is a sign that we're ready to evolve. My mom used to joke, "Wouldn't it be nice to just have a chicken brain and not have any deep thoughts?" And while I don't think any life is an easy life, not everyone will experience a radical shift in consciousness in their lifetime. But when your number comes up, it's kind of like it's your turn to get on the Tilt-a-Whirl. So, buckle up, here we go!

Shift Is Getting Real

So now that we've covered the why and the how, let's move on to the "what the hell?!" Signs you are experiencing Deep Shift may include increased anxiety, confusion, and restlessness; a fierce knowing that something needs to fucking change; a newfound love of nature; sleepless nights; the feeling that you are going insane; the feeling that EVERYTHING is changing; a desire to live totally differently than you have been living; a craving for simplicity; becoming an introvert when you were always outgoing; supernatural abilities like being able to communicate with animals; psychic abilities; and even some other super wild stuff, like literally being able to make yourself disappear (more on this one later!).

Whew. Basically, you "woke up" in Opposite Land—a place where the old rules no longer apply. As you can imagine, however, a lot of these symptoms get labeled "crazy" or "scary" because they are so outside the norm. We aren't used to feeling or thinking this way, and it can be very overwhelming and confusing, as if you're starting a new life in a new country but you don't have anyone to talk it over with. Especially if you start having "peak experiences" (more on these later). That heightened sense of wonder is incredible, but you need context and an understanding of what is going on in order to integrate it. While what you are experiencing is totally cool, it can also fuck with your mind. Please do not freak out: You are not alone in this (even though it probably feels like it right now). I will be your friend and guide.

Even better, when we get used to it, many of us discover we are actually old pros at this; we've just caught a case of temporary amnesia. We are all born "awake," after all, but over time it's brainwashed out of us. Life beats us down, and next thing you know, all sorts of magical things that we used to take as a given seem completely alien. But the magic hasn't gone away; you simply lost the ability to see it. You forgot that it exists. Now, in the advent of a particularly significant life event, cracks begin to appear in the carefully constructed, protective glass facade of our life, and the truth begins to reveal itself again. It may take some time and handholding to integrate all of these new ways of being into our current reality. But the cool part is that this universal knowledge is built into our cells. We already know how to do this, to live differently and on our own terms—it just takes a little elbow grease to get the wheels turning.

The first step is to tune out the external noise and tune into our inner voice and inner knowing. This in itself takes practice, time, and attention, as you may have to prove to yourself that what you believe to be true is real. Actually *acting* on what we know to be true and right for us, versus what society and other people in our lives think is best for us, often requires ninja levels of courage and focus. It also means you may find yourself going against the grain, living differently than you were taught. You are now officially on "the road less traveled" (thank you, Robert Frost), and this means some time must be spent preparing for how to do this thing called "an awakened life." The pot of gold at the end of the rainbow? We start to make decisions based on our own desires, we begin to think for ourselves, and we carve out the life that lines up with our True (with a capital *T*) selves.

By the way, the concept of having a radical personal awakening and becoming a full-blown Shifter (more about *them* in the next chapter) is as old as the day is long. People have been taking this journey since the beginning of time. From Eckhart Tolle to your next-door neighbor to ancient religious figures, enlightenment and the path of awakening to your authentic self is available to all of us, and it always has been. In my humble opinion, we are born to take this ride; we are made for ch-ch-ch-changes, deep shifts, and radical transformations.

As you are beginning to experience for yourself, what I'm talking about is so much more than New Age mumbo jumbo. Deep Shift is the doorway to a profound breakthrough in a person's life and an unmistakable inner revolution. And no, I'm not talking about a self-help manual to losing fifteen pounds or switching careers or making time to take more naps, either. This is about becoming a *whole new person*, from soul to skin. A major shift in consciousness from the deepest levels of your being. *Two lives for the price of one!*

Bottom line? When you embrace your inner Shifter, it's as if you realize you ARE MAGIC ITSELF. Buh-bye boring, frustrating, unfulfilling life! Hello to having "the Force" running through your very veins. I mean, what could be more empowering than having God as your business partner, the Universe as your relationship coach, and the energy of the Cosmos at your back? So, get ready to officially lose your shit and let's get into it. Welcome to Deep Shift. Your very own new normal is waiting just around the corner for you.

Five Signs You Are In Deep Shift

1. **Your interests completely change.** For example, if you were once a party animal, now you find yourself wanting to stay in and be alone. Or you'd always been "gung ho" about being a city person, but now you can't get enough of being in nature.

2. **Your relationships begin to change.** That old group you used to hang with no longer holds your interests. You want new friends who can really "see" you. This also refers to romantic relationships. You find you're seeking more substance in your partnerships. Anything less just won't do.

3. **You have a strong urge to switch careers.** The desire arises to pursue work that moves you, instead of just showing up for a paycheck. Your purpose in life becomes clearer, and you realize that taking a job because it's convenient or "the money's good" just isn't going to cut it.

4. **You become less materialistic.** You find yourself less and less interested in accumulating things. Instead, you're drawn to living in a simpler manner. Less clutter, less chaos. Inner and outer peace are at the center of your ambition.

5. **You feel a sense of calm.** You're reassured from within, knowing you're made of the same stuff as the trees and squirrels. You come to realize (or at least glimpse) your connection to or oneness with the Universe. That everything really is as it should be and there are no mistakes. Living in the present becomes increasingly desirable and effortless to experience, a blessing unto itself.

CHAPTER 2

What Makes a Shifter?
(That Is, Why Me?)

"Every act, every word, every thought of ours not only
influences our environment but for some mysterious reason
forms an integral and important part of the Universe."

Irina Tweedie

So, what exactly is a Shifter? This is my term for those among us *lucky enough* to experience being in Deep Shift, which can happen to any of us. However, in my travels and over the many, many long conversations I've had with other deep Shifters, I've also begun to notice a pattern. They tend to be highly sensitive, highly intuitive, and highly spiritual. They're often into nature and all kinds of mystical anything: from spiritual practices to clean living, astrology, psychic abilities, creativity, and the arts. They're also typically operating on an altogether different wavelength from the rest of the herd, are what you might call "built for growth," and tend to experience life as a process of almost constant transformation. As such, Shifters are constantly learning and growing—Deep Shift being the Big Kahuna wake-up call that comes along any time they have gotten "stuck."

So, is a person born a Shifter, hard-wired for a life of evolution and growth that is the essence of their true path? Or is a Shifter made by the experiences life throws their way?

I believe it's a little bit of both. Often, it's going through Deep Shift that opens a person who might otherwise have gone through life like a total normie, to a more, shall we say, alternative worldview. Others might come to this path through a gradual awakening to the mysteries of the Universe, or perhaps they have witnessed (and helped) somebody close to them go through the Shift. And sometimes, we Shifters are born this way and have been on the path to "enlightenment" (or "awakening" or "self-realization" or whatever works for you) our whole lives.

Another trait I've noticed among Shifters, however we arrived in this place, is that many of us experienced some kind of trauma at a young age. In my case, I was so sensitive that I could feel everyone's emotions. As any empath knows, this in and of itself is traumatizing. Throw in two passionate parents, a brother with schizophrenia, and plenty of general life drama, and lo, a lifelong Shifter was born. When you grow up in an environment that's abusive or highly unstable, your intuitive abilities also become sharp as a tack. For many, it's a survival tactic, born from a need to always be alert for danger and to be able to read people at the drop of a hat. This adaptation can be part of what opens us up to higher states of consciousness.

Shifters also often have "delicate" nervous systems. This can prove challenging, in that they can be hypersensitive, touchy, or easily affected; nonetheless, this trait also makes them keenly sensitive to the people and the world around them. This means that once a Shifter gets their nervous system under control (a must, and something we'll be addressing in-depth in Chapter 6), they have the ability to become true sages, great teachers, and laser beams of light in the world. Left unchecked, an extreme sensitivity can result in panic attacks, fear, and uncertainty at every turn.

What makes a natural-born Shifter?

- Spiritual experiences occurring at a young age

- A superb eye for detail. People may often remark, "You see everything!"

- Extra sensitivity to noise, people, the "energy" (positive or negative) in one's surroundings (or people), food, and alcohol/drugs

- Easily overstimulated

- Thrive within a simple, low-stress lifestyle

- Can easily become ill if surrounded by negative energy in people or food

- Great empathy for people and animals

- Deep connection with and love of nature

- Thrive working alone or running their own business (i.e., instead of working with a group in an office environment)

- Drawn to the unseen world, spirituality, astrology, psychics, meditation, yoga, mysticism, and/or religious practices

- Can get depressed or anxious more easily than others (i.e., those with "thicker skin")

- When not maintaining proper balance or health, tend to be codependent and put themselves in second place

- Often need more rest, down time, and alone time than others

- Loathe small talk (hence, can struggle in their relationships)

- Feel EVERYTHING deeply

- Can be very extroverted, yet also have social anxiety

Many Shifters share some of these traits with empaths and Highly Sensitive People (HSPs), the latter being the term coined by psychologist Elaine Aron to describe those among us who feel alllll the feelings and can't help but live life ocean deep. But a true Shifter is also hardwired for what

I call "peak experiences"—or radical shifts in consciousness. For example, while empaths have the ability to feel other people's feelings, a Shifter will take it one step further through their ability to connect to a Higher Power and download Universal information about any given situation. Born with direct connection with the Cosmos as the guiding light in their lives, Shifters basically have the ability to go a bit Star Trek on everybody's ass.

If you suspect this might be you (um, it's very likely you), then you are about to discover that all of the above is GREAT NEWS! When Shifters come into their power, meaning when they tap into the stream of grace that naturally exists inside of them, they become wizards. Yes, I said *wizards*. Simply put, they embody a spiritual edge that can bring them inner fulfillment, high self-esteem, true mastery of their personal power, and the ability to think and live entirely on their own terms. As well as being an example for others on how to master the game-changing art of *"waking the fuck up."*

However, unsurprisingly, society doesn't really know what to do with us Shifters, the result being that we're often actively discouraged from exploring our true natures. Because guess what? Once a Shifter learns to live their life their way, the scales begin to tip, causing the rules, systems, and programs society has set up to wobble and topple like a house of cards.

To prevent this, the programming starts at a young age. Yep, despite the fact many of us operate on a very different frequency from everybody else, we're taught how to think and behave in a world that frankly isn't set up for Shifters. The traditional path of getting straight A's, going to college, getting on the corporate ladder, getting married, having 2.5 kids, and living in the burbs, in that order, just isn't going to work for a Shifter. Or maybe that's all been working out just GREAT . . . and you don't relate so much to the above. But like I said, Deep Shift can happen to anyone, and if you're reading this then chances are that the winds of change have come a-knocking, and everything you've spent your life diligently working toward has been blown away like a house of cards in a hurricane.

Whichever way it's been for you, focusing all our energy on worldly matters siphons the magic right out of our systems, and once that happens, well, things aren't going to go so well. Continuing to try to fit in when you're living in Opposite Land will eventually lead a person to a breaking point, forcing one to carve one's own path and break away from the herd. Often, the only way we can undo our conditioning is by going inward, doing the work, and embracing the gifts we were given. Enter Deep Shift— that is, the kind of life-altering experience that's designed to get us back in touch with our Shifter roots. The good news? This book has all the tools that anybody needs to navigate Deep Shift.

If you get the sense that you are in the thick of it, the sooner you can start marching to the beat of your own drum, the better. Also, the more Shifters you can connect with, the more fulfilled you're going to be. The good news is, once we're in the Shift, we can often "see" each other. We understand where one another is coming from, and there's something very comforting about being in the presence of other Shifters, a sense of acceptance we may not find elsewhere. It may not feel like it right now, but you are not alone, my friend. There are lots of us out there, and once you know how, you'll be able to spot us pretty darn quickly.

When I look back, I can see I had Shifters on both sides of my family: a Greek aunt who had profound visions in her dreams; an Irish cousin who had a near-death experience that changed her life in an instant; a brother who was such a Shifter, he psychologically went over the edge; and a mother who was a full-blown Shifter and embraced it to the fullest.

That's right, being a Shifter is often in our blood, passed on from generation to generation. My family is that way, and many Shifters I've met, talked to, or read about have said the same. Given how Shifters have been overlooked or outright repressed, the missing piece in our Shifter heritage, more often than not, is "the rules of the game." As in, how to be a Shifter in a rule-book world and crush it in your own Shifter way. "Work with what your mama gave you," they say. In my case, I'm lucky in that my mama gave me the treasure map to the road less traveled. The way of the Shifter!

A Shifter Is Born

As you know, my mom was a very powerful influence on my life. As far back as I can remember, she filled my soul with ideas about how to live a magical life, cultivating the Shifter in me. For example, her views on education were vastly different from those of most other parents. She had always been in school herself, right up until six months before she passed away, enthusiastically taking classes in mysticism, writing, and political science at the University of Chicago . . . for fun. Yes, *fun*. The interesting part is that she never actually worked toward a degree! While most people frame their diplomas and hang them in their offices (the better to define themselves by), Mom could have cared less about that coveted piece of paper. For her, education simply brought joy and nourishment to her spirit. She studied at her own pace, picking courses that interested her most, and moving through school (and life) on her own terms, like the Mama Shifter she was.

And my mother passed her passion for learning and books down to me. Before I was nine years old, we'd regularly take trips to cool bookstores and have amazing adventures. A typical experience would find us at a used bookstore in a funky part of town as our first stop, followed by coffee for her and a huge malt for me. We'd talk about the books we'd picked out and the ideas that stemmed from them. Simple. Enlightening. Transformational. Any Shifter's ideal Saturday!

School became more challenging for me as I grew older, but my mom always had my back. She would always say, "You have your whole life to be an adult. Be a kid; be carefree and just have fun." She didn't feel like kids should have stress in their lives or deal with the crap adults have to put up with. She read me Shel Silverstein books, took me on adventures, and let me be me. She never laid a trip on me; she wanted me to be authentic and happy. Period. By the time I got to junior high, I was spending countless hours devouring inspiring biographies and spiritual books to feed my fascination with the human mind, body, and spirit. I was growing into my Shifter ways and tapping into a natural curiosity that led me to see what the unseen world had in store for me.

My mom essentially showed me with both her words and actions that the way everyone else was living was not the *only* way. She was the opposite of a pushy, demanding "tiger mom." I was expected to get my chores and homework done, of course; but in our house it was public knowledge that my report card would never define who I was. She was more interested in raising a strong daughter who had a sense of self and was free. My mom wasn't concerned with what society wanted or expected. And since magic was at the center of her world, it was important for her to make sure that my life was filled with light, love, and happiness.

With this attitude, she was essentially showing me that a Shifter's life is a *slow* life (apparently, we were precursors to the slow living lifestyle movement waaaay before it was a "thing"), that competition and goals are for suckers, and that it is in nobody's best interest to become bogged down by stress (public enemy number one of the Shifter). Her big message to me? To *enjoy* my time on this planet.

Part of my mother's brilliance was in listening to her body. When she was tired, she simply took a nap. When she was hungry, she ate exactly what she was craving. Mom didn't deprive herself of sleep, food, rest, or her passion: writing. Yep, writing was her priority, and during her life she published three books and had her poetry published in many poetry journals—and if that meant keeping odd hours so she could get her "work" done, so be it.

She often would bring a coffee and a bag of Dunkin' Donuts munchkins with her into her back-of-the-house office at 10:30 p.m., when my brother and I were going to sleep, where she'd write until 3 a.m. She had an agreement with my father: she would write at night, and my dad would get us ready for school in the morning so she could sleep in. That's just how we rolled. We all supported Mom's writing, even though she wasn't getting paid for it. It was her joy. Period. What a brilliant example of how to get your Shifter priorities right.

And on the subject of priorities, she also didn't buy expensive clothes or jewelry, as that stuff didn't interest her. In fact, she sewed most of her own clothes and mainly dressed in black. Getting ready in the morning is a whole lot easier when every piece of clothing in your closet is one color! I used to tease her that she was the female Johnny Cash, her favorite singer. What I didn't realize at the time was that she kept her life as simple as possible in order to keep her nervous system in check, and so that she could always stay true to her authentic self.

For all Shifters, turning to a Higher Power (or as they say in the twelve-step programs, "a God of your understanding") seems to come naturally, and a built-in curiosity about "what's out there" often kicks in early. Shifters have a natural connection to their spirituality and are drawn to the mysteries of the world. That's their playground. I lucked out because I had a mom who was already swimming in those waters.

Prayer and meditation, too, were a major part of my mother's life, and her spirituality was always at the top of her list. She knew that a slow and simple life, filled with God, was the key to contentment. And now I see that this is precisely what gave her an edge. Her spiritual edge. Mom leaned back and relied on her Higher Power—which was, for her, the rushing, flowing energy streaming from the Universe—to carry her through her life. She very naturally passed down this information, this way of being, to her daughter, and in doing so, beautifully set the stage for my future self. Yet like many of us, somewhere along the journey, I lost my way.

Because guess what: the way of the Shifter is not all grilled cheese sandwiches and chocolate malts. At times, it can be absolutely, earth-shatteringly insane and heart breaking. Given that Shifters feel *everything*, until you go all David Hawkins and get your consciousness calibrated to a higher number, any time the world and the people around you suffer, you are going to suffer. Screaming kids, college loans, endless to-do lists, traffic, complicated relationships, health issues, political turmoil, social unrest, and too much caffeine, sugar, and fast food can cause tremendous amounts of stress, disease, and general hell-on-earth conditions for a highly sensitive Shifter. This is why it's essential to develop a way to stay on top of your nervous system. Get this part right, and you can actually use these experiences for what you're built for—*to grow*. To teach you that since you aren't in control here, you might as well do yourself and your nervous system a big old favor, and let go and let God.

Which Comes First, the Breakdown or the Breakthrough?

In my own life, the stress monsters began to gain traction around my mid-teens. Note to reader: I share what comes next to convey that I know hardcore levels of stress, anxiety, and overall hellishness. But fear not! After a few examples from the trenches, I'll go straight into how to use your Shifter ways as a powerful means for transformation, regardless of what challenges you're facing.

When I was fourteen my brother, Peter, had just begun his freshman year of college at Salve Regina, in Newport, Rhode Island. My mother's close friend, Sister Sheila, was the president of this amazing university and a major reason Peter chose to attend. The campus looked like a fairytale on the Atlantic Ocean, and its students were extremely privileged. My brother immediately made friends with some well-off kids and fell into a fast-paced lifestyle. He flew on private jets and regularly went to Manhattan to fill his weekends with parties frequented by models, actors, and socialites. It was the kind of high-end life he'd never even dreamed possible.

Peter's sophomore year, however, proved to be very different. I'd just turned fifteen, and one evening I was sitting in the living room with my parents when the phone rang. It was my brother, calling from school to talk to my mom. I remember her exclaiming, "Peter, what are you talking about?! You are *not* being followed by the mob!"

What. In. The. Hell. Was. Going. On? The look on her face was one of horror, and I found myself staring deeply into her eyes as she tried to talk my brother down off of a mental cliff. My heart began racing, and a deep, dark confusion set in—a terror that would stay with me for the next twenty years.

Peter had snapped. One minute, he was a thriving college student who had life by the tail, and the next he was my out-of-control brother having a psychotic breakdown. He would go on to be diagnosed with schizoaffective disorder. Never again did I experience my brother as being "normal." This major shift in our family changed everything. Gone was the bohemian, laissez-faire lifestyle I once knew and loved. Everything became extremely serious, with one "Peter explosion" after another. Psych wards, psychiatrists, medicine, fighting, and chaos became our new reality. Then, within five years of my brother's diagnosis, my mom was diagnosed with stage four breast cancer. The stress was literally killing her, and there was nothing I could do to help. In fact, most of the time I felt like I was just trying to come up for air.

At that point, I was working sixty- to seventy-hour weeks running one of my dad's restaurants in the suburbs and bartending at a wine bar in the city, while also grappling with a terrible sleep disorder and sky-high anxiety levels. And yeah, I was self-medicating the whole time (and I'm not talking about aspirin and Alka-Seltzer).

This went on all through my twenties and into my thirties, until my mother passed away. It felt like fate had robbed me of my peace, vitality, well-being, and creativity, as well as my ability to think rationally and make good decisions. It was as though I'd become just another hamster on a wheel, running in circles to nowhere, with zero connection whatsoever to the life it had felt like it was mine to live. As for my Shifter gifts? I had pushed this part of my life away completely as I focused on trying to lead a "normal" life.

All I could focus on was keeping my mom alive and keeping my brother sane. In my own life, I was desperate not to be single, I was desperate to make as much money as possible, and I was desperate to have a huge social life. That's right, I was *desperately lost.*

Obviously, this was no way to live. But honestly, at that point, I felt I didn't have a choice. Adding to her battle with cancer, my mom was up to her ears with my brother's issues, all while Dad was trying to keep his business afloat, and virtually everyone I knew was running around like a chicken with their head cut off. For a Shifter like me, it was both dizzying and toxic. I remember rationalizing to myself, "This is just how life is and will always be: *hard.*" Working until your fingers bleed, saying yes to every invitation, and settling for a partner who might be (just) "okay." I couldn't see any way out, blinded by both stress and my fast-paced lifestyle, sinking even faster than I could understand, and numb as to how I could help myself.

When my mom passed away in 2011, *my* house of cards came crashing down. Years of unacknowledged trauma, of ignoring my own needs, and truckloads of stress crushed me to the ground. I hit absolute rock bottom, became suicidal, and completely shut down. My mind, body, and soul were like, "Yo, we out!"

Yet, as you now know, it was *only as a result of* this traumatic breakdown that I was prompted to learn how to meditate—the experience that led me into Deep Shift and squarely back onto the path of the Shifter. Sitting in my bedroom alone one day, I *almost* swallowed a margarita glass full of pills. I stopped myself from going through with it, though. And it wasn't until that very moment that I flashed back to how my mother had raised me. What she had shown me about how to tap into the flow of magic in my life. How to slow it down. How to simplify things. How to let stress roll off me, and actively choose the thoughts, activities, and way of life that made my nervous system hum.

Once I'd learned how to meditate, had slept for a month (as in, I literally slept for a month, straight), and gotten my feet back on solid ground, I began to understand again how easeful and good life could really feel. That this human existence could be calm, peaceful, *and* full of transformational magic.

TF for the Simple Life

And all of this is waiting for you, too, on the other side of Deep Shift. You may not be able to see it yet, but what you're experiencing is actually in service of you tuning in to your higher self. The real you! Chances are, you are being stripped of relationships, beliefs, and ways of being that you've developed as a defense mechanism against life. And while this feels like a shitshow right now (trust me, I know!), the Universe is essentially bringing you back to basics. Remember what I said about Shifters needing to learn how to regulate our nervous systems? Living a simple life, with as few bells and whistles as possible, is essential to our well-being.

For example, after learning to meditate, I quit my restaurant job and started working for the David Lynch Foundation. I gave introductory lectures on TM, led group meditations, and was on hand to talk to new meditators about their lives and their experiences. But even this wasn't a simple enough life for me, and two years later I decided to sell all of my furniture and most of my possessions, rent out my condo, and move to the countryside in Iowa. This is where my true appreciation of simplicity and slow living kicked in. The very first night I spent in my new home (on fourteen acres in the heart of the Midwest countryside), I could literally feel the shift in my mind and soul. As if my insides were expanding to match the outside, and the stars in the night sky were also inside of me. In the silence, I also felt my mind and nervous system completely calm down. And with the calm came the gifts.

It has become clear as day to me that there's a direct correlation between a calm nervous system and staying in the flow with God/the Universe/Great Spirit/whatever you want to call "It." The quieter I got, the more powerful my attention and focus became. The more I cut distractions out of my life, the more I accomplished. I felt unstoppable . . . in a very *quiet* way. As if a limitless energy was running through my veins, which I was free to channel into the things that *really mattered to me*, I felt the incredible sense of peace that my mom had exuded.

Of course, not all of us are in a position to quit our job, move to a cabin in the woods, and go all Walt Whitman, but the beauty is we really don't need to. What we *can* do is begin to take inventory of our lives by noticing what's working *for* us and what's working *against* us. We can take a good, honest look at what's causing us stress and thus keeping us disconnected from our own inner knowing. We can begin identifying the emotional or behavioral issues we've often learned to rely on to "cope" with being our sweet, sensitive selves, and get to work on unwinding them, one by one.

Of course, sometimes we get handed a set of circumstances that turns our life into a living nightmare for us. But remember what my mom used to say: *"The bad never stays bad forever."* And from my experience, it doesn't.

Because, as you are beginning to understand (loud and clear, I hope!), it's often during the nightmarish times that we can have our biggest breakthroughs. I firmly believe life is not random. When you're a natural-born Shifter, things are set up for you to awaken to a larger reality and a more expanded consciousness. Often, this is only possible once we see our mirage of success, or even happiness, get washed away by tragedy. This is when we are forced to slow it down, to tune back into the grace of God/the Universe, and to show some love to our inner Shifter. It's when everything starts to fall back into place.

Are You a Natural-Born Shifter?

Because I'm curious (and I bet you are now, too), let's see if you identify as a natural-born Shifter. That is, somebody who is basically here to transform. To do this, answer each of the following questions to the best of your ability. Take a moment after you read each question and check in with your gut. Answer yes if the question is more or less true for you. Answer no if it isn't true at all for you. More than 50 percent yesses . . . and we have ourselves a Shifter! And if this isn't you? Well, you are definitely here for a reason. And in the coming chapters we'll be finding out exactly what that is.

Can you pick up on other people's emotions easily?

Do you feel sensitive to loud noises and/or bright lights?

Are you strongly affected by caffeine, alcohol, and/or processed foods?

Do you feel very connected to animals?

Would you say that you have a rich inner life?

Do you need alone time on a regular basis to get centered?

Do you generally feel highly intuitive?

Do you find yourself "playing small" in order to accommodate other people's inability to go deep?

Do you often feel like an outsider? Unrecognized or unseen?

As a child were you always being told you're too sensitive?

Do other people's moods affect your sense of well-being?

*You are doing great! Keep going, you are halfway there.

Do you get overwhelmed with changes in your life?

Do you have problems sleeping?

Do you have a hard time making decisions?

When you get hungry do you feel REALLY hungry—to the point that you can't think and are in a bad mood?

Are you naturally drawn to spirituality or connecting with the unseen/unknown side of life?

Do you have or have you had deep spiritual experiences?

Do you have a hard time with relationships—bouncing back and forth between feeling too much or feeling nothing at all?

Do you sense you are a "healer," naturally able to assist others with their personal healing?

Does the idea of working in an office or a crowded environment make you uneasy?

Do you feel exhausted after interacting with a sick or distraught person?

Do you feel irritated if you are asked to do multiple tasks at once?

Do you find it difficult being in big cities/around a lot of commotion?

Do you find yourself attracting narcissistic partners?

Do you sometimes (or often) think you're crazy or that something is wrong with you? (You are so *not,* by the way!)

CHAPTER 3

Everything You Think You Know Is Wrong

*"When I let go of what I am,
I become what I might be."*

Lao Tzu

In the summer of 2011, I sat down with my Transcendental Meditation teacher in Chicago and was taught how to meditate. Nothing in my life could have prepared me for what I was about to experience. A complete transformation, in twenty minutes flat. Body, mind, and soul broken wide open. Ready for a new whole human to emerge. I didn't even have the thought, *What the hell is happening?* Instead, the realization that hit me was: *Everything I thought I knew was wrong.* I even uttered those words out loud when my meditation teacher stepped back into the room. There wasn't a shadow of a doubt that everything I had learned from my religious studies training and my years studying spirituality, and all my thoughts about how things really worked, was ALL WRONG. Not only wrong, but backasswards.

In learning to tap into that deep silence inside of myself, I flipped a switch. The "Opposite Land House of Lights" came on and I was no longer in the dark; I was seeing with new eyes and hearing with new ears. As I sat in the meditation teacher's office, the children playing outside sounded like angels. Outside her window, Lake Michigan was a vivid blue green I had never seen before. Like waking up in Disneyland, it was as if my state of awareness had kicked itself up about fifty notches; I was experiencing an elevated state of being that would change everything for me.

Over the coming days and weeks, everything felt heightened. It was simultaneously like being on drugs and being more sober than I had ever been. Colors, sounds, tastes, and smells were more vivid. I became obsessed with trees—I could feel them breathing! And the depression and suicidal thoughts that had followed my mom's death were replaced with a sense of total calm as everything slowed down and I became saturated with the present moment. It was trippy as fuck.

Little did I know, though, how quickly this would also find me questioning everything about how I thought my life "should" look, what success meant, and what would make me happy. Like most of us, I'd believed that success was the result of hard work, and that the ultimate goal was to make a bunch of money, get married, and have kids. I also believed that I had to dress and look a certain way to be accepted. Overnight, none of this stuff mattered; somebody could have dropped me off in a forest and I would have been fine. When I subsequently lost people in my life, I was even happy for them—I totally "got" that death was just another natural life transition. It was as if I had so much trust in life that I had lost all fear about things not turning out "right."

Could I ever have prepared myself for an experience like this? Of course not! The rules of a sudden spiritual awakening can't be taught in school. It can be discussed, we can read books about it, and the hallmarks of the experience can be laid out in front of us; but until we actually experience it for ourselves, no words can do it justice.

It's like trying to explain what a papaya tastes like to someone who has never eaten one. They can see pictures of a papaya, and they can even feel the texture of one or smell its aroma. But until they actually take a bite of a juicy papaya, they will never really know what it tastes like. Up to that point, they can only have an idea of what a papaya tastes like. It's just not the same. Having a spiritual awakening is the same deal. You have to taste it to truly understand.

However, does that mean you don't continue devouring information on spirituality? Not at all. Each and every Shifter was born curious about the Truth, with a capital *T.* We can't help but be seekers. It's in our blood.

And the more we know about the nature of a radical personal transformation—including how to prepare for or navigate it—the better off we'll be when it inevitably happens.

These types of experiences may take weeks, months, or years to unpack. What's basically happening is that you are starting to see how much has been "programmed in," versus you living as the "real you"—resulting in you completely transforming who you thought you were and totally shifting gears. But this "Holy shit, what is happening?" level of change doesn't happen overnight. And while navigating the choppy waters of Deep Shift, having as much information as possible at your fingertips will help things go much smoother than if you were starting from ground zero.

That being said, you can only go so far with "external" knowledge, and it should be viewed as more of a support system than a substitution of the actual experience—including what I share with you in this book! Nothing in the world can replace the lived experience of "awakening," directly experiencing the Source/the Universe-as-Yourself, and all that comes with an adventure this momentous!

For example, in the midst of a Deep Shift, we can have very unusual experiences, like suddenly knowing *everything*. Yes, you heard me right: knowing EVERYTHING. When I found myself in Deep Shift, not only did I feel like everything I thought I knew was wrong, but I simultaneously felt like the secrets of the Universe had been lying dormant in the cells of my body and were now waking up.

It was like I no longer had to use my mind to "figure stuff out." In my first book, I even went so far as to declare that "thinking is overrated." Instead, it was like the Cosmos was showing me what to do, by reminding me that I'd been here and done this life thing a million times before. I had knowledge I didn't even know was there, most profoundly the sense that there is actually no such thing as "right" or "wrong," "good" or "bad." There just "is." Nothing in my religious upbringing or spiritual studies to date could have taught me this newfound level of acceptance, which is ultimately what helped me to trust that whatever decision I made or path I took, it was always the "right" one for me. In fact, the reason they don't teach you this in church is that if we all knew this, there would be no church!

With all the changes that were occurring, it was clear to me that there was one way to live on this planet; I had to go rogue, to move in a different direction and essentially start doing the *opposite* of what everybody had always told me to do. And since this is what's worked for me, I'm going to teach you how to do it too. From my experience, when you're in Deep Shift you'll greatly help the process along by adopting a warrior stance and going ALL IN with whatever life is throwing at you. What I would go on to learn was that not only is doing the opposite of everyone else often the only way to go, but it is also a way to kick some serious ass without losing your mind. Allow me to explain.

It's Not You, It's Them

Let me be clear: ALL of your relationships are going to change after you find yourself in Deep Shift. You will look at your friends, family, coworkers, and anybody else you come into contact with differently. And not only will you "see" people differently, noticing their emotional responses—their pain and their joy—as much as their physical appearance, but they will also sense the changes in you. The good news is you will probably be able to deal with all the changes and transformations you're experiencing better than the other people in your life. The not-so-good news is that people tend to get a little spooked when they see somebody growing like crazy. Your friends and family may not know what to do with you. For example, if you've always been a "life and soul of the party" kind of a gal, the first time you turn down an invite because you'd rather stay home and read a metaphysical book, stand back and watch the shit hit the fan!

The bottom line is that most people don't like change, period. It's destabilizing and has a way of revealing all the holes in a person's carefully curated worldview. Which means *you* being in Deep Shift and showing all the holes in the matrix means the *other people* in your life are going to freak the fuck out. Get ready for it.

The best friend who can no longer relate to you and gives you a hard time about your life choices. The family member who thinks you're completely off your rocker for something as simple as changing your diet or your sleeping habits. A boss who can't understand why you've either totally lost interest in your job or are getting your work done at warp speed. On the surface, it may seem like everyone you know is losing it over these seemingly small changes. But the reality is they are spinning out because, consciously or unconsciously, they can feel that your energy has completely and fundamentally shifted. And they don't know how to handle it. At least, not right now.

So how should *you* handle it? It's time to get realistic—not everybody in your life can come with you for this ride. As for who to keep in your life, let me break it down:

1. Feel your way forward with each relationship. Ask yourself, "What makes this relationship important to me?"

2. Decide how much shit you can handle in order to keep the relationship intact.

3. Know when to walk away. Some people are likely going to give you a hard time, and "If you love someone, set them free" should be your motto in these circumstances.

4. Give yourself and the people in your life time to get used to the new you. Remember, you are now vibrating on a different frequency than them, and it may just take them a moment to catch up.

5. While you wait, keep reminding yourself that *they can't see what you see.*

6. Don't force it. Just keep doing you and allow your presence to lift up the people around you who are ready. The new energy you're running will spread out of you like a cosmic rainbow.

Remember, everyone is on their own path. It isn't your job to educate anybody or to convert those who don't "get it"—the ultimate goal is to find and align yourself with people who are already cruising down the same spiritual highway as you. This might mean finding a whole new gang over time, but these are the relationships that will satisfy you, fill you up, and help you integrate all of the new information you're receiving into your system. They are your soul family, and you will know them by the way they make you feel.

Actually, now is the perfect time to really start paying attention to this. Ideally you want to feel energized by the people you spend time with. Inspired, interested, curious, and filled with joy. What you don't want is to feel wiped out, confused, anxious, or angry. The feeling and the energy you experience in the company of others will tell you everything you need to know. So, raise your antenna around everyone. Carry a notebook with you and jot down how you feel about a person you've just had contact with. Make sure you date it, so you have a frame of reference. Later, I'll show you how to protect your energy in any type of situation and how to stay in your lane while still allowing love from others to touch you. (Note to self: "We want to let the love in and keep the bad juju out.")

As for how being in Deep Shift impacts romantic relationships? This can be a tough one on many levels. I've seen people drop-kick their marriages, long-term relationships, and dating as a whole after they find themselves in Opposite Land. Which makes sense. Our romantic partners are the people who know us the most intimately, and so it makes sense that this is one area where the shockwaves of your transformation will be felt the most intensely. For example, people who once couldn't spend an evening alone may suddenly crave solitude. Others who'd always felt content being the stay-at-home type now want to go out and join a softball team or become a public speaker. It's these great deviations from a person's norm that can be the most shocking, especially to the people they're in relationships with. Yikes!

Imagine being in a relationship with someone who no longer shares the same reality with you. It would be like living with an alien! You can hang on for a while, but unless your partner grows with you, it's going to be nearly impossible to stay in union with that person. Especially when the type of partnership that's going to satisfy you now that *everything you thought you knew is wrong* will no longer be a McDonald's quarter-pounder-with-cheese kinda hook-up. You're going to need the relationship equivalent of lobster thermidor.

In my case, I've felt a strong pull to remain single until God, the Universe, the angels, and my deceased relatives bring me the right person. No substitutions. Shocking, I know! This is the opposite of my norm; I'm the kind of gal who's had a boyfriend since as far back as I can remember. But I am no longer a lady who has to be in a relationship. The time I've been able to spend alone or with friends who can really see me has made me more independent, wiser, and bolder, and has left me with a sense that *I complete me.*

Not least because being in Deep Shift found me in deep partnership with my*self.* Meaning, doing an in-depth examination of my life and how I wanted to walk this earth. In the process, I became fearless, going on solo adventures and devouring books, talks, and other information on spirituality and transformation. I took myself on retreats and solo vacations, went skydiving, and did a bunch of public speaking. Along the way, I began meeting totally groovy people all over the world, completed a master's degree in spiritual psychology, wrote two books, and started a business I love. The bottom line is, I entered into a relationship with myself and with God, whereas before I had looked outside myself for fun, excitement, and validation.

It also became clear that I could ONLY be in a relationship with somebody who was on the same page as me. My writing career even began with a blog titled, "Settling in Love or Life Is Not an Option." I had decided I would no longer settle in any area of my life, because it was clear *I didn't have to.* Being in Deep Shift and having your whole world turned upside down can be one of the most challenging experiences there is, but it also sets you free from the bonds of everyday life. The upside of everything looking completely different is that you get to do everything completely differently! With no set script to follow, the present moment literally becomes the most important thing. And it is staying in the now that allows you to feel whole. Nothing in the external world can complete you like being connected to yourself and to the Universe can. And this includes relationships, or the lack of one. You are complete, just the way you are. If a partner pops into your life on top of having a deep love affair with the Universe, well, then you've got some *extra* icing on the cake.

To me, romantic love is a mysterious alchemy—and can even be its own gateway to Deep Shift. Love can drive us to move across the globe at the drop of a hat, or turn our backs on previously held obstacles, boundaries, and expectations. And yes, in some cases, it can even feel like we are "crazy in love"!

When we encounter true love, the cosmic meeting-you-feels-like-coming-home kind of love, everything is heightened, and life can take on a whole new meaning. This alone tells me love is a Divine force in and of itself, with the power to propel us headfirst into Deep Shift. With a love like this, the beloved becomes a clear mirror that allows us to see everything *we* are. Including the parts we don't always want to see. This alone helps us to evolve as individuals in wild and wonderful ways!

But still, it begins with you, and when you are in Deep Shift you become highly available for the kind of no-holds-barred self-love that, in my view, is essential groundwork for any lasting and authentic romantic relationship. Oh, and my definition of "self-love"? I believe this is the result of turning your attention inward and tending to whatever you find there that's been crying out for your attention for, like, ever. Which *any* Deep Shift will require of you. Learning to give *this* inner self the love and validation it needs is how you learn how to give and receive love from another.

Is It All in My Head?

Another part of the puzzle we just can't ignore is the impact of being in Deep Shift on our mental health. Not only can shit get pretty "cray," sometimes we can really get thrown off our game, feeling like the ground beneath our feet has literally been swept away. In fact, at times it may feel like you are completely losing your marbles. And we don't want that for ourselves or anyone else.

Addictions, repeating patterns of self-sabotaging behavior, or just the fallout from years of wear and tear on our minds, bodies, and souls: all of it will now come up to be addressed. But when we are experiencing so many changes at once, coupled with the lack of understanding from the people around us, it can be hard to navigate our way in the midst of a Deep Shift. Let alone find solid footing when all hell appears to have broken loose.

The thing is, any and all challenging experiences or "breakdowns" can actually be the doorway to breakthroughs. But you'll very likely need some support in order to get hold of the reins before your anxiety level skyrockets or things get too out of control. Although I'll be sharing plenty of tips and guidance for this throughout the book, you may find yourself needing additional support, and I encourage everyone to seek help where they need it. For now, one of my favorite quotes that has really gotten me through some tough times is from Hunter S. Thompson. He starts off his 1971 masterpiece, *Fear and Loathing in Las Vegas*, by stating, "When the going gets weird, the weird turn pro."

And let me tell you something: the very fact that you are in Deep Shift, with the going suddenly getting weird as hell, means you are ready to "go pro."

What does this even mean? Often, the inner chaos or moderate-to-severe freak-outs that can arise during this process stem from unresolved past traumas being triggered by your Shift and rising to the surface. In this case, going "pro" can literally mean it's time to seek some professional help to process all of this. If you are a natural-born Shifter—which, as we've established, I'm pretty sure you are—then you will very likely have had some traumatic experiences in your life. Possibly many. If you've already begun your healing work on these, more power to you. But if anything from your past remains an obstacle to your awakening, and in order for you to truly know yourself and your reality, then NOW is the time to find a fantastic therapist and . . . Do. The. Work.

Navigating this new mental landscape is a bit like learning to drive a stick shift: you have to know when to ease off the clutch, when to shift into a higher or lower gear, and when to pump the breaks. Ideally, you'll have a good instructor to guide you in this process. It could be a mentor, a super-wise friend or family member, a therapist trained in or experienced with transpersonal psychology, or an "awakened" teacher or college professor you've relied on in the past for insight. The point is, having someone in your corner you can turn to for all things "personal transformation" will make the road forward a whole lot smoother (and less shocking or scary)! The good news? Once you've begun awakening into this more expanded state of awareness, you'll likely move much faster through any unresolved past pains and hurts. You'll also be inclined to grasp new perspectives, ideas, and philosophies more quickly; have a deeper understanding of why people may have acted the way they did; and—what may be the greatest gift of being in Deep Shift—become a clear-eyed witness to your life.

As you become more familiar with the experience of being in Deep Shift, it becomes easier to see the motivations behind what may have been hurtful or abusive behaviors (or attitudes) of people in your past or present. Having a more cosmic, insightful perspective can help you find acceptance and at times even forgiveness of those people, allowing you to move forward more freely in your own life. But often enough, the seasoned "outside perspective" of a keen-eyed and compassionate counselor, family member, mentor, twelve-step sponsor, wizard-friend, and so on is necessary to help you heal unresolved past wounds and climb over any internal hurdles.

In Deep Shift, talking it out with somebody else can make any old stories that contributed to past patterns you stayed stuck in less "sticky." And you're then able to let go more quickly of whatever's not working for you while at the same time identifying, practicing, and integrating healthier behaviors and attitudes. Also, with the expanded awareness and larger lens through which you're viewing life (i.e., as you get used to it and eventually master it), you'll see yourself facing and handling relationships and situations that used to negatively trigger you in the past with much greater ease and freedom, while remaining true to yourself and the Cosmos flowing through you.

Bottom line? You want to put some space between your daily awareness and the emotional charge of any unhealed past traumas. This is one of the most powerful benefits of meditation. With that daily deep-dive into your essence, plus getting in regular sessions with a kick-ass therapist, you can learn to exercise your ability to step back and look at any traumatic or triggering situations with fresh eyes. Instead of reacting, you can begin to respond by leaning back. In this way, you enter into a space where you're no longer being controlled by your emotions. You're no longer a leaf in the wind. You are now the fucking tree. Your roots are deeply planted in the ground.

My Body, My Temple

Let's now move on to physical health. When you find yourself in Deep Shift, you will, without a shadow of a doubt, feel different about how you treat your body. Many people become vegetarians after having a spiritual awakening. No longer can they tolerate the suffering of animals for their personal consumption. "Do no harm" is a mantra that seems to emerge in the hearts of awakened humans—and this absolutely applies to your food and other consumer choices. Not only when it comes to how they will affect you, but the animals, the environment, and society as a whole. Think big picture.

You may also become sensitive to various foods that never bothered you before. The fact is, you're running on a new system now, and this means paying attention to what choices support your nervous and digestive systems. That "fuck it, I'll eat whatever" mentality ain't gonna fly anymore. I personally found I could no longer tolerate caffeine, dairy, gluten, or more than a couple glasses of wine, mainly because I was no longer willing or able to put up with feeling like shit! I was ready to respect my sensitivity, which also manifested as sensitivity to certain foods and other lifestyle stuff, as I now knew it was a SUPERPOWER. Some of this has to do with age, but a large portion of it has to do with a refinement of my system. Now my body craves pure, fresh food; and when I don't give it what it wants, it lets me know. Don't be shocked if this also happens to you. It's par for the course when you start treating your body right.

I even went so far as to experiment with fasting, which I knew to be a practice for clarifying the body and mind. It does this by detoxing the system, helping break addictive patterns, and giving your digestive system a much-needed timeout so that you can really *feel* the emotional debris that's often stored in the gut. Now, fasting definitely isn't for everyone, and there are certainly other methods to explore what foods and patterns are affecting your digestive health, but fasting was what worked for me. Fasting taught me how not to use food (consciously or unconsciously) as an escape or a way to avoid my feelings in the moment. The same way meditation helps us become the observer of our thoughts, fasting helped me see my eating habits more clearly, helping me become aware of where I was out of control, when I used food as a crutch, and how to use food as fuel.

During my first fast, I didn't eat solid food for twenty-one days. Yup, you read that right. No food. TWENTY-ONE DAYS. But this is not me telling you to go cold turkey and dive in unaccompanied if this is something you are looking to explore. Anyone interested should work with a professional so they know exactly what they should be doing.

As I was finishing that fast, I realized that we not only cleanse our bodies with fasting but also cleanse our senses and our spirit. Fasting, or another type of elimination system, such as Whole 30, can help clear your mind as you get to experience all your "gut feelings'" in the raw! The result is that you feel more spiritually and emotionally connected, and your perception of everything is more intense.

I also noticed that when it came to my health, things like homeopathic remedies, acupuncture, energy work, and massage really helped me, and I became more interested in preventative medicine than relying on medication. Rather than stick a Band-Aid on it, I wanted to get to the root cause of any issue that came my way—be it emotional, physical, or spiritual. I was connecting to my body on a different wavelength, and I knew that the more I could get out of the way and let it do its thing, the better I would feel.

What's the Point?

So, as well as all of the above, it's likely that everything you thought you knew about your purpose in life, your career, what success means to you, and who you want to be while you are on this planet also just got turned on its head. And I mean upside down and backward. So, it's time to dig deep and start uncovering how you *really* want to do this thing called Life. And if you're lucky, the Universe will drop some bread crumbs and show you the way. Your job will be to pay close attention and take the necessary action steps to get on the right track. *Your* track.

When I had my Deep Shift, I could not in a million years have foreseen what was to come. Up to that point, I was in the restaurant and bar business. My idea of a good time was staying out till 5 a.m. and hitting up as many clubs as humanly possible. My vision of success was being wealthy, having a large group of friends, having a well-to-do husband, and traveling all over the world. You know, the basic American Dream with a good-old splash of today's consumer culture thrown in.

Then the Deep Shift happened. On the heels of losing my mom, everything changed. None of those old ideas about how things "should" be even crossed my mind. I wasn't interested in any of it.

Overnight, it seemed, my interests shifted instead to one sole purpose. To help people.

I went from pulling in a six-figure income and working sixty- to seventy-hour weeks, to working for the David Lynch Foundation (DLF) and making $11 an hour. And I had never been happier. Every day, I got to go to work and talk to amazing people like Oprah Winfrey (I mean, okay, pretty special), executives, people in medicine and finance, plus tons of school children, about happiness, peace, and consciousness. As far as I was concerned, I had landed my dream job. This is why I was on the planet . . . *and I knew it.*

The "old me" would never have discovered this. I would have balked at making that little money, not trusting it would all somehow work out, and I would have robbed myself of one of the greatest experiences of my life: I would have never fallen into the pool of magic that I now found myself swimming in *every single day.*

The far-reaching green lights I gave myself to *just go with it* during this period changed the entire direction of my life. I wouldn't be writing this book today if I hadn't taken a leap of faith and said HELL YES! to the road less traveled. Was I scared? Yes. Did I know that this was all going to play out as amazingly as it has? I did not. Did I do it anyway? Yep! And, boom.

But I wasn't alone. Working for the DLF meant I had a community of other spiritual seekers around me. People I could turn to when the weird got even weirder. Their examples inspired me to make changes and take chances. I did the necessary soul work as it arose, as I saw it calling to me. And I'm *still* doing the work to this day. The only difference *now* is that I *know* everything will work out.

Yes, your relationships, your mental and physical health, and your approach to your work and purpose are all going to be upended while you're in Deep Shift. But any changes that are occurring are about bringing the dynamic, interconnected system that is YOU back into alignment, so that you can go forth and live your life in the most cosmic, super-smooth way possible. Sure, the process of transformation can seem long and filled with unforeseen forks in the road. But the golden treasure at the end of the rainbow is that you are always being led back to you. Your true self. And there ain't nothin' better than that.

If you're in Deep Shift, you are ripe and ready to have the Universe as your partner in crime and source of Divine guidance. You don't NEED what you used to know. Next up, it's time to find some solutions and systems that work for YOU to help you stay the course—so let's look at getting you hooked up with some kind of a map.

part two

Welcome to Opposite Land

CHAPTER 4

Shifting Up a Gear

"Things which matter most must never be at the
mercy of things which matter least."

Johann Wolfgang von Goethe

O kay, so you've woken up in Opposite Land, and everything you
thought you knew was wrong. You are quite likely encountering some
truly challenging—and I mean *Uncomfortable* with a capital *U*—emotional
and even physiological responses to the major changes that are occurring in
your life. I'm here to tell you that with some careful planning, and the right
tools, *it doesn't have to be overwhelming.*

The thing is, by the time you're in Deep Shift, *the change is already happening.*
It's your job to keep up with the pace and look after yourself as best you can.
And while there's no point trying to second-guess where all this is headed, it is
essential to have touchpoints in place to help you keep your feet on the ground.

Easier said than done. When I was in Deep Shift for the first time, I would
sit outside for hours just staring at the trees. The color of their branches, the
sound of the wind in their leaves. . . . It was as if nature had taken on a whole
new vibration, and it was intoxicating! It would have been so easy for me to
just float away in my own bubble of bliss. But that would not have been any
good to anyone. To stay being a person in the world, I needed to find tools
to keep me in the here and now.

Navigating Opposite Land and making the Shift work for you is about
staying in reality while also allowing the supernatural to flow through you.

This means staying focused and taking action on whatever's coming up for you, while also staying open to hints from the Universe about the next choices to make and actions to take. Instead of having to have your life all planned out (I mean, how stressful is that?), the synchronicities are all lining up and now you're being *shown* the next steps in each moment. And with one foot essentially in two worlds, it's important to find ways to stay balanced.

Over the next few chapters, I will be introducing something of a Shifter tool kit—essentially a box of tricks for surviving and thriving while you're in Deep Shift and the world as you knew it morphs and shapeshifts in front of your very eyes. First and foremost, this means being able to orient yourself on your path, no matter what kind of a shit show may be going down. Before we dive into the nitty-gritty, here are three simple steps to ground you as things Shift up a gear.

Where You At?

I will often ask people, friends and clients alike, "On a scale of 1 to 10, 10 being the worst, where are you at with that?" You'd be surprised how much I learn about a person from this simple practice. It's a habit I picked up spending so much time in hospitals with my family members, and I discovered it's also a great way of gauging my own feelings and determining "where I'm at."

Asking *yourself* this question about any important situation or dimension of your life can be a great way to recognize where you stand, as well as being an illuminating guide for you as to what's "the next right thing" to do. This exercise forces you to pay attention to what's actually happening in your life—and where you need to direct your Shifter energy next. Because of the excellent results it's gotten me, this simple practice is one of my favorite journal exercises. It's hard to bullshit yourself when you're using this method, because let's face it, the numbers never lie.

With the ch-ch-ch-changes coming thick and fast, as relationships morph and shift, and old interests and #lifegoals begin to fall by the wayside, it's the perfect time to use this technique to take a look at where you stand and where you're being called to go from here. Not only will this help the Shifter in you get crystal clear on where you stand, but it will also help you make a plan for you to "Shift-proof" your life so you can sit back and roll *with* the changes versus being blindsided by them.

The "dimensions of life" I list here can offer you a good starting point—and you can add your own as they arise or occur to you. Respond to each one of these questions with a number that reflects how you honestly, authentically feel, right now, using a scale from 1 to10: 10 being "It's real bad" (i.e., time for some DEEP Shifts!) and 1 being "I'm so happy I could float away."

How do you feel about your career?

How do you feel about the area where you live?

How do you feel about your home?

How do you feel about your closest relationship (i.e., husband, wife, boyfriend, girlfriend, child, if applicable)?

How do you feel about your eating habits?

How do you feel about your friend group?

How do you feel about your relations with your family?

How do you feel about your daily routine?

How do you feel about your spiritual practices?

How do you feel about your life in general?

Now, you can work backward. Let's say you sat back and really thought about your career, got a 10, and realized you are 100 percent in the wrong field. You feel totally stuck, like you have to get the hell out of there, STAT. Like, if you have to go into your current place of work one more day, you're going to lose your goddamned mind. No if, ands, or buts about it, you need to find a new job. Not just any job, though—one that *really* drives you, something you love, a career path that aligns wonderfully with your new way of being.

Now, this might sound like a tall order, but when you're in Deep Shift you have the Universe at your back. Things can change in a heartbeat, and your job is to stay open to the signs and say yes when the opportunity arrives.

This same "walking it backward" approach can be applied to any area of your life. This exercise can help you identify those areas that are calling out for more attention, some significant adjustments, or a complete overhaul. And, by the way, no need to feel guilty or ashamed about any of it. This is all about making your Deep Shift, your own personal transformation process, as complete, righteous, and rock-solid as possible, one step and one day at a time.

Remember: while everything might feel like it's falling apart (especially if you gotta lotta 10s up there), we are Shifters, people. We've been put on this planet to transform. This means putting ourselves in the driver's seat of life and jibing with the rules of the universal consciousness, *not* the rules of society. It's also our job to show others how it's done.

"So what's next?" you ask. Simple. It's time to go back to the drawing board, or in this case, the writing board: your private journal.

There is power in writing things down. I never leave my house without my favorite notebook and my pen of choice. Yes, I am a grown woman and I have a favorite notebook: a light-gray journal made by Notem, a design agency in Copenhagen, Denmark. And I use a Pilot G-2 gel pen, in the blackest of black. I won't use anything else. Why? Because my journal is sacred to me. It helps me stay organized, helps me make major decisions in my life, holds all of my creative ideas, *and* is my most trusted confidant. My journal knows all. I treat it with respect, and, in turn, it guides me down a really groovy path.

Let's stay with the example of your current job being a big fat 10. (Again, you can apply what I'm saying here to any area of your life that's clearly needing change!) There's no more denying it. The work you do is no longer working for you and it's time to make some moves. We Shifters always follow our gut, but we also think things through. Tap my intuition, write it out, make it happen. That's my jam.

When assessing the lay of the land (Opposite Land, that is), it's important to get clear as a bell. Which now means it's time for some more questions. For example, what are your options? If you could have things be exactly the way you needed in this particular zone, what would that look like? Who do you know that can help you? What will living that new path look like? And my personal favorite, "What beliefs do I need to put aside to become the person I want to be?" They say the divinity is in the details, right? Leave no stone unturned.

And if you're anything like me, getting your thoughts organized on paper and then *talking it out to myself out loud* helps it all come together. When I hear myself say things out loud, they seem to make more sense to me. I am able to marry the emotions I feel with the words that are rolling off my tongue. Yes, I am literally recommending *talking to yourself*—as in, saying everything you are thinking out loud to help you feel into your gut instincts about it. For instance, if I say out loud, "I think it would be fun to go back to bartending," but then I get a sick feeling in my stomach or my heart starts to race, and not in a good way, I know that isn't right for me.

Intuition, writing it out, action. This combo is a triple-threat to a tired old status quo that's being swept aside by the tides of Deep Shift. Write it down, say it out loud, and then watch for the answer to appear, based on how you physically feel.

You want to change your daily routine? Gauge where you're at on the 1–10 scale. Write down exactly how you want to feel, then write a step-by-step plan about all the different ways to help get your ass there. All good spiritual practice comes back to discipline: you may feel like you want to swim with the stars, but when you're in the midst of massive change, you have to stay focused and grounded. As ancient Chinese philosopher Laozi wrote: "Don't think you can attain total awareness and whole enlightenment without proper discipline and practice. This is egomania. Appropriate rituals channel your emotions and life energy toward the light. Without the discipline to practice them, you will tumble constantly backward into darkness."

And the same goes for showing up for your Shift when it comes to the big changes in your life. When you're in Deep Shift, the change is already a-coming—and the best way to roll with it is to commit to whatever follow-through is necessary to make that change stick. If you resist the Shift, God (literally will) help you. Meaning, the Universe will step in and knock you down, over and over, until you get with the program. Your life is no longer your own; with the Universe calling the shots, it's time to let go of the reins and see where life leads you. The sooner you realize this the better.

Being the Witness

So here we are. Washed up on the shores of Opposite Land, with our lives lookin' a whole lot different. Having asked some probing questions, answered them honestly, and tallied up the results, there's probably at least one area—if not many—in which we know the old ways will no longer cut it. The good news is that Shifting is our game; when we lean into this and let go of the need for control, it comes naturally to us. But we can also learn to play the rules like a pro.

For example, witnessing. It's time to learn it, live it, love it.

So, what is this "witnessing," and how will it help you get your transformed ass in gear, without losing your marbles in the process?

Simply put, witnessing is the ability to zoom out and look at your world through a neutral lens—and it is one of the hallmarks of higher consciousness. It's essentially what a good therapist will help us do; while in meditation, it's known as "observer equanimity"—or "detached observation." Instead of being all IN your thoughts (which feels as if your thoughts "are you") you are now overseeing your thoughts from a "higher" consciousness (your thoughts are now more like a movie you are watching). Learning how to be the witness in all of your affairs likely won't come to you overnight. But with some supportive counseling and bringing forward your own spiritual and psychological elbow grease, you can get there. The best way I can describe it is that you feel as though you're watching a movie, except that the movie is your life. You are observing all the characters, places, and scenarios in your reality, but you aren't attached to any particular outcome or being emotionally controlled by *any* of it.

Rather than reacting as if you're watching a car crash in slow motion, when you're in witnessing mode it feels like you've settled into a cushy armchair with a big bag of popcorn and are watching the film that is your life from a grounded, calm, and gentle perspective. If you've ever had this experience, you will immediately recognize what I'm talking about. This is especially important when you're in Deep Shift as it also saves your nervous system—because if we Shifters are anything it's *sensitive*. In TM it is described as "no longer feeling like a leaf in the wind." Sounds relaxing, right?

This is not the same as avoiding or repressing any experiences or feelings that feel too challenging to confront head on. Rather, it's as if you're fascinated by your life—totally engaged with whatever is unfolding in front of you, but without being blown all over the place and becoming worn out by it.

Even knowing that this state of awareness is available to you gives you an opportunity to consciously lean back. For example, when you find yourself getting overwhelmed by this or that, it's time to stop, drop, and become the witness. Remind yourself that this moment, no matter how wild and confusing it feels, will surely pass. That it is just one more experience to add to the other five billion experiences you will have in this lifetime.

Another one of my favorite quotes (which has stuck with me for years) is from Aldous Huxley's final novel, *Island*: "It's dark because you're trying too hard," said Susila. "Dark because you want it to be light. Remember what you used to tell me when I was a little girl. 'Lightly, child, lightly. You've got to learn to do everything lightly. Think lightly, act lightly, feel lightly. Yes, feel lightly, even though you're feeling deeply. Just lightly let things happen and lightly cope with them.'"

Huxley perfectly captures the feeling of being the witness of your own world. Of not feeling the need to grip hold of any particular outcome. Of just going with the flow and letting the universe work through you. This is the freedom that witnessing can give you.

The first time I had this experience, I was standing in Oprah Winfrey's screening room at her studio in Chicago. It was my first day working at her company, Harpo Studios, for the David Lynch Foundation. I had absolutely no clue what I was actually going to be doing, having only been told, "Walk in that room and tell your story." Looking back, it was probably better that I *didn't* know my audience would be Oprah HERSELF and her then right-hand person and studio president, Sheri Salata. Yep, just the two of them.

Now, one might think it would be completely terrifying to, out of the blue, be talking with Oprah about my transformational meditation experience on some random Monday morning. At that point I hadn't done any public speaking since my eighth-grade speech class. It's not like I was some polished orator, but what I *did* have was the ability to witness.

I introduced myself, and Oprah asked me to share my experience with her and Sheri. What came next was the most surprising part of the whole deal, at least to me. I had *zero* fear. I could see the words coming out of my mouth before my mind was even registering what I was saying. It was as though someone or something was speaking through me and I was just the observer.

I also recognized another amazing aspect of this state of witnessing, which I had been cultivating in my meditation sessions and which now arose organically: Oprah and Sheri were just two women sitting there—who I'd never met—but I instantly felt as though I had known them my entire life. It felt easy, peaceful, and fulfilling to talk with them, and I felt absolutely no judgment of myself, my words, or either of them, the entire time. All I felt was straight-up consciousness and truth running through my veins.

When I was done, Oprah looked at Sheri and said, "I want what this girl has!"

I then calmly said, "You will have it. Just keep meditating and it will come."

And that was it. I ended up working at Harpo Studios for two years, speaking every week about consciousness, happiness, and meditation to groups of Oprah's staff before and after they learned TM.

My new career had picked me.

Why am I telling you all this? Because when you're operating at a higher state of consciousness, which is what can come on the heels of being in Deep Shift, the Shifter in you "remembers" the supernatural gifts that have been lying dormant in your system. Witnessing is one of them, and you can begin to train yourself to do it simply by stepping back and widening your lens on life.

In *Polishing the Mirror: How to Live from Your Spiritual Heart*, Ram Dass describes the simplicity and naturalness of the state of witnessing: "The witness is your awareness of your own thoughts, feelings, and emotions. Witnessing is like waking up in the morning and then looking in the mirror and noticing yourself—not judging or criticizing, just neutrally observing the quality of being awake. That process of stepping back takes you out of being submerged in your experiences and thoughts and sensory input and into self-awareness."

Dass continues, "One simple way to begin developing the 'witness' within your daily life—besides learning and practicing daily any meditation technique—is to take moments throughout your day when you consciously step into 'observer' mode." For example, if you find yourself getting frustrated because you're stuck in traffic, take a breath, and picture yourself floating above the car and witnessing the whole situation that's causing the jam. While you're in line at the checkout, imagine you are watching yourself: how are you standing; what's in your basket; are you fidgeting? The more you practice gently detaching and becoming the observer of your experiences, the more you will slip naturally into this state and the less caught up you will become in the daily dramas of life.

The gift of witnessing also is a perfect tool to use when your personal transformation is shifting into high gear. It allows you to look calmly at your life, see where the changes are taking you, and take action without feeling overwhelmed. Witnessing helps you to stay neutral. To not get overly emotional about what may be ending and where you may be headed. It's your grounding gear and can help you Shift-proof your existence.

Find Your Person

Now let's add another helpful resource to the mix. When you're in Deep Shift, the changes can come at you thick and fast, especially as relationships in your life morph and shift. With everything up for grabs, it's time to home in on what really matters to you—in terms of work, family, relationships, and the wider arc of your life path.

One key ally I've found tremendously valuable is a "sounding board" person, someone who can listen to me share what I'm experiencing and then expand my way of thinking about the important questions that arise. Someone who can help me zoom out to consider the lasting impact of the changes I'm experiencing, as well as the choices and decisions I'm making.

As you are in the thick of Deep Shift, this person will ideally have no agenda except to help you be happy and succeed. This usually requires someone outside of your closest group of friends and family. Let's face it, the people closest to us can't always "see us" without some old story getting attached to their lens. This means they will likely try to keep us as we were *without even knowing what they're doing*, simply because they can't see us any other way. They don't know what to do with the "new you"—it will blow their circuits! This is not their fault, and it also doesn't mean they are "less evolved" than you. It just is what it is.

While you may feel drawn to talk things out with your bestie, a better bet may be an experienced therapist (referrals from respected friends or loved ones can be a good place to start), an insightful life coach, a twelve-step sponsor, or a spiritual counselor. Preferably, you want to connect with another Shifter, so they truly understand where you're coming from. Remember: when you cross paths with another of our kind, you will often know. Bells will go off in your soul almost instantly.

And also remember, there are many free resources that can get you started and help you find others to support you on this journey. I've found amazing Facebook and MeetUp communities full of people on a similar path to me at various stages in my Shift. Perhaps your local community center or church offers free or donation-based yoga, or other therapeutic classes. Text therapy is a new development that's made professional help way more accessible. And if you are in a position to pay someone, make sure you're honoring them as you'd like to be honored.

Why? This kicks off the partnership from a place of mutual respect. It sets up a mutual desire to do some really great work together, and it's also a reflection of how I want people to treat me. When you begin working with other people, it's very important to serve them as you would want to be served. By treating others well, you're actually showing the Universe how you want to be treated, respected, and honored. Do right by the people who help you, and the Universe will do right by you.

Get God/Big Bird on Speed-Dial

Okay, to recap, using the 1–10 trick to journal on what's up (and what's NOT), becoming the witness of your life, and seeking some experienced, insightful, and supportive outside help will all help you stay on track and roll with the changes that are streaming into your life. These three practices alone will bring clarity to any situation.

The final piece for staying grounded in your Shift is to have faith in the ways of your Higher Power/God/the Universe. Which basically means *connecting to your body*. Given what we're often taught about the supernatural nature of "spirit," this is probably not what you were expecting me to say! But the truth is, your Higher Power/God/the Universe communicates primarily with you THROUGH your body—meaning, by the way your body feels in any given situation.

A super-powerful exercise that we are *not* taught in school is to check in with your body daily: asking yourself, how does my body feel in this situation? To do this, all you have to do is get quiet, zone in, and wait to see what pops into your mind: you will *always* get the intel you need if you ask your body what you need to know. This makes your body your instrument for connecting to God on a daily, ongoing basis. And since being in a physical body is the opposite of floating away with the fairies, this is also a great way to stay grounded on the daily.

Any time you find yourself faced with a moment of overwhelm or uncertainty, take a moment to sit and get quiet and just be with the physical sensations in your body. You may need to sit in another room, take a bathroom break at work, or pull over and just sit in your car for a moment.

As you feel into your body, be aware of what thoughts, memories, and visions come to the surface of your awareness. What message is coming through? Are you feeling tight in your chest or stomach, is your heart racing, are you feeling goosebumps up your arms? If the sensations are overwhelming, try pausing to take one full, deep inhale, hold it for a moment, and then let it slow-w-w-l-y out of your nose until you feel completely empty. In the moment of calm that follows this, pay attention to the physical signs your body is giving you. On an even more simple level, feelings of levity and euphoria are a green light. It's a go! And on the opposite end of the scale, feeling heavy or anxious about something is a sign that it's not aligned for you right now (even if logic says differently). The next step is to trust what you are feeling and then act accordingly. Easier said than done, but I promise by the end of this book you'll feel more confident in your ability to trust your instincts.

Life is an adventure for everyone, but especially for anybody who has entered Deep Shift. We are no longer playing by the same rules as everyone else. We're led primarily by the laws of the Cosmos, which means letting our inner guide take the wheel. And we do best when we follow our gut feelings and bodily cues right into our destiny. Even if this goes against what society (a.k.a. our family, friends, boss, etc.) would have us do. Allowing yourself to live this way may feel like unfamiliar territory to you—even be scary, at first—and it very well may take you on many unexpected, off-the-beaten-path journeys . . . but the more you lean into it, the more natural it will feel. You may even come to see being in Deep Shift as your natural way of being, and the old way as having been restrictive to who you truly are.

Your body may help you decide, "You know what, I'm totally over living in a small apartment in a big city. I'm going to build out a van and make the road my home." Or it may have you admit to yourself, "I've always wanted to be a writer. I'm going to shit-can my soul-sucking job, get a part-time gig, and spend my free time following my passion."

Now, I'm not telling you to drop-kick your entire life over a hunch, but I *am* saying . . . that might be what happens. And there is nothing wrong with that. What is important is to keep one foot in reality, get the support you need, and stay grounded in your body, so you don't become overpowered by the sheer force of the changes that Deep Shift can bring into your life.

During my Deep Shift, I found myself doing so many things I would *never* have imagined possible. But the more I let go and leaned into the changes, the doors just kept opening, leading to more and more outrageously cool experiences, connections, and happenings. It was having a strong connection to my Higher Power that meant I felt safe to keep saying a big HELL YES! to each and every opportunity that came my way. My mind was no longer the pilot of my life—my *soul* was. And this made life a whole lot cooler! I became an adventure junkie, and my everyday reality became infused with pure magic.

For example, checking in with how my body felt about it was why I said HELL YES! when the opportunity to go skydiving in Santa Barbara one morning revealed itself to me. That one yes about *jumping out of a plane* happened to lead to me having lunch at one of the most incredible restaurants I have ever eaten at, where I ran into the actor Emilio Estevez, who then invited me to a party at a local winery, which then led to a speaking gig at that same winery a couple months later, which led to me going out on my own for more speaking work, which led me to selling everything I owned and moving to the country, which led to me writing my first book, which then led me to doing more life coaching, which then led us here. See what I mean?

All of this because I got a call that morning asking, "Hey, ya wanna jump in the car, drive to Santa Barbara, and go skydiving today?" To which I was able to reply HELL YES! because the pulsing green light in my body said it was a goer.

And this is what I want for you, my fellow Shifters. The freedom to open up to new perspectives (using the 1–10 journaling technique); the ability to calmly show up for what's in front of you through witnessing; the insightful guidance and empowerment of having a solid sounding board in your life; and a rock-solid connection to the intuitive, Universal, God-shaped guidance that's streaming to you through your body every day. Instead of freaking out about all the Shifts that are hitting the fan, I want you too to be able to say a solid HELL YES! to the adventures that are going to present themselves to you.

And trust me, they are coming. That's what makes being in Deep Shift as magical as it can be painful. You're opening yourself up to a whole new dimension of reality. And as my mom often told me, "God can think up a way cooler life for you than you could ever imagine."

The tools I have laid out here, as well as what I will introduce in the following chapters, are what will help you stay open and move through life with the innocence of a child. One of the hallmarks of higher states of consciousness—and a feeling that can be the result of going through Deep Shifts—is a simple knowing that all is well. For you, for the world, and for all of God's creatures. When a person is vibrating at a lower energy level, there can be a tendency to think the world is going to hell in a handbasket. But that simply isn't true. It's just conditioning (not to mention a super-manipulative media machine) that makes you see the world that way.

Not that there won't always be suffering in the world; the suffering never ends, and if anything, being in Deep Shift helps you to accept it as just another part of life. But mindset is EVERYTHING when it comes to how you approach it. For example, after I experienced Deep Shift, I was no longer destroyed every time there was another death in my family. I could accept death as part of LIFE, and even be happy for the person who was passing. Turning the pain to power? Now we're talking seriously higher octaves of consciousness, baby!

Once you pierce the veil of illusion and peek behind the curtain, you'll be in no doubt that the world is a magical place and that you can live a truly extraordinary life—no matter what your circumstances.

One of my favorite writers/people in the world is Father Richard Rohr. In one of his books he shares an experience he had as a child. It was Christmastime and he was sitting in his living room, staring at the lighted Christmas tree. He said, "I had the sense that the world was good, I was good, and I was part of the good world—and I just wanted to stay there. It was like being taken to another world—the *real* world, the world as it's meant to be, where the foundation is love and God is in everything."

Now that's a Deep Shift in consciousness if I've ever heard one!

And also? It's hard to be a high-vibe person and hate anybody. The feeling that the world is my family, and that help is around each corner, makes it easier to let the Universe guide us and to trust that everything is happening just as it should be. This is perhaps the most beautiful by-product of going through Deep Shift. And yes, it may also be ground zero for the way you want to be living your life in general and where you want to be making decisions from going forward.

Not from a place of fear, but from a place of freedom. And this is what this book is for. With some introspection and some good guidance, you could soon be living a life you never thought possible. This is just the start of your new reality. Pay attention to where your soul wants to lead you. Dig deep and find out what YOU really want and then *do that*. Clean up your side of the street, and then walk right into your destiny. Chances are, it has been waiting for you for a very, very long time.

CHAPTER 5

Fill Up at the Meditation Station

"When meditation is mastered, the mind is unwavering,
like the flame of a candle in a windless place."

Bhagavad Gita

h aving a regular meditation practice is very important for the Shifter. Actually, let me rephrase that. Meditation is *the most crucial practice a Shifter can incorporate into their life.* Why? Well, for the Shifter (and for all people really, but especially anybody wading through Deep Shift), the external world isn't where it's really at. It's our *inner world* that feeds us, that allows us to tap into the wonder and magic of being, and that fuels our creativity. This is where we fill up on the juice of life, and meditation is the vehicle that pulls us up to the pump.

Which is also, you guessed it, the opposite of everything we have ever been taught.

Indeed, our parents, teachers, and society have raised us to look *outside* ourselves for, well, everything. We're taught that everything we need to be happy and feel safe and secure is outside of us: whether it's good grades in school, a college degree, a high-profile career, fancy clothes and vacations, marriage to "the one," 2.5 kids, or a retirement condo in Florida. But my experience has shown me quite the opposite: *Everything we're looking for is inside of us, and meditation is the key that unlocks the door to the limitless Universe lying deep within our souls.* It is the number-one practice to have in your Shifter tool kit. This is especially important to remember when we're going through Deep Shift, as it's very likely that a lot of the external stuff has been stripped away, leaving us feeling (emotionally at least) naked and alone.

The other cool thing about meditation? It slows everything down and gives us space to *be the witness* (aha!). When you meditate, you're essentially training your brain to give you a break already from the constant stream of thoughts in your head and the constant emotional reactions these thoughts trigger in your body. When the changes are coming thick and fast, the thoughts and reactions speed up too, and before you know it you're on a fast train to Anxietyville, wondering how everything's going to turn out and trying to prepare for all the worst possible outcomes. Exhausting!

When the Shift is hitting the fan, a regular meditation practice is exactly what you need, as it allows you to take whatever's coming your way at your own pace and meet life on life's terms. If Deep Shift shows us anything, it's that we are NOT the ones pulling the strings around here—and that the more we try to control the outcomes that are unfolding in their own magical (if sometimes painful) way, the more stressed out we get.

The good news? Not only does meditation calm and settle the nervous system through a meditator's eyes, but you start to accept things as they are. Viewed this way, and without your fight-or-flight response getting hijacked every five minutes, challenges become opportunities. You can handle whatever curve balls come your way with clarity and grace. Instead of freaking out about the grocery store being out of toilet paper, you will have more space for what's really important: creativity and connection. The irony is that this actually puts you *back* in control. Not in control of what's happening, but in control of how it makes you feel.

Scriptures from around the world underscore the truth and importance of this perspective. In fact, every major religion highlights the importance of looking inward for spiritual connection and, ultimately, a shift to a deeper, more expanded consciousness. Here are a few examples:

According to the Bible (Luke 17:21), Jesus told his disciples, "The kingdom of God is within you," while also saying (per Matthew 6:33), "Seek ye first the kingdom of God and His righteousness [i.e., go inward and meditate], and all these things shall be added unto you [you'll get everything you want!]." In the Bhaddekaratta-gatha (a sutra, or teaching, in the Samyukta

Agama, the oldest known collection of Buddhist teachings), Buddha said, "Looking deeply at life as it is in this very moment, the meditator dwells in stability and freedom." And in the *Tao Te Ching*, Lao Tzu explained, "To a mind that is still, the whole Universe surrenders."

Taken together, these ancient precepts not only sum up the purpose of meditation but also provide us with guidance about "the basics" of the practice.

First of all, in meditation we're directed to turn our attention inward and embrace the silence and stillness that is always beneath or behind the seemingly endless stream of thoughts. To be clear, these thoughts are what keep us stressed out all the time, racing along the hamster wheel of life. Now, you begin to see that thoughts are just stress in mental form, and that thinking is NOT how we "figure things out." Meditation teaches us that the answers are in the silence, and that the more we can just sit back and DO NOTHING, the more the Universe shall provide! Again, this is the opposite of what we've been taught.

You can imagine your everyday thought-filled consciousness as a wave on the surface of the ocean. When you meditate, you're allowing yourself to drift down and become one with the silent depths of that vast ocean of universal consciousness that connects all things.

The way I see it, silence is the language of the Cosmos—because when we're silent we can hear what the Universe inside of us has to say. If our body is how we interpret the messages, then becoming conversant with the silence *within us* is how we learn to hear God/our Higher Power speaking to us . . . and it works *like magic*. By redirecting our attention from the outside to the inside, we're turning away from the noise and distractions of the outside world and toward God/our Higher Power or whatever, a.k.a. the source of all the contentment and bliss we humans can handle.

The Basics

The basics of meditation are really pretty . . . basic. Meditating simply means quieting the mind and sitting in silence. When we do this over and over again through regular practice, we start getting familiar with the unbounded ocean of silence within. Over time, our daily meditation stimulates the silent depths of our unconscious mind, and all sorts of information, which has been waiting for us in as-yet unmanifested form, can then begin to emerge and stream into our awareness. And when I say "information," I don't mean the names of all the TV shows from the 1960s. I'm talking about valuable stuff, like what's *actually* triggering us in our relationships with others, or how to move forward in the best, most fulfilling way imaginable in any given situation. Result!

Once again, for the people in the back: *this* approach to living life— or problem-solving or dating or how to "be healthy" or . . . (you get the picture)—is the *opposite* of everything you've been taught up to this point. While everybody out there is scrambling around looking for the next guru, app, or life hack that's going to miraculously solve all their issues, meditation takes you on an *inward journey*—and *this* is where you'll find all the answers you're looking for (as well as some you didn't even know you needed to hear).

What I've come to see is that it's actually the *distractions* in our lives (including the gurus, the apps, and the life hacks) that keep us confused, anxious, and all up in our heads. Meditation is like a washing machine for the crazy stuff. Just like psychologists say you process information in your sleep, when you meditate, you're tapping into a part of your mind that you don't normally access that can help to transmute any frustration, confusion, angst, or pain you may have been experiencing.

Which sounds pretty epic, right? And pretty much like exactly what you need in the midst of a neck-Deep-Shift-storm. If you become too attached to any pain and anxiety you're experiencing, it will take you down with it. This is not the same as avoiding or bypassing anything that's coming up. Rather, it's about making space for it all to be there, without attaching to it or letting it completely derail you and rob you of your agency.

So how does it work? In layperson's terms, meditation is designed to keep bringing us back to our *true nature*. What do I mean by this? I believe that all humans are born calm, happy, loving, nurturing, and giving—and that over time we just get ground down by ALL THE THINGS. When we meditate, we get to touch base with the essential self that's always been there underneath.

You can also think of the mind as an onion, with each layer representing another set of beliefs, old traumas, and old conditioning. In meditation, you get to peel back each layer of your reality—as all the pain, the happiness, and the desires that are embedded in the old wounds and resentments, as well as the good and bad memories stored in our brains, are allowed to rise to the surface in the form of *thoughts*. Y'know, the pesky opinions, judgments, and directives from your ego that like to tell you how the world is going to shit, everybody's out to get you, and that you're a terrible person to boot.

So how exactly does a person meditate?

There are actually two main camps when it comes to meditation: mantra-based meditation and mindfulness meditation. I practice Transcendental Meditation (TM)—which falls into the mantra-based camp. This means you repeat a special mantra (a word or phrase) in your mind as a way to detach from your thoughts. Any time you notice yourself thinking, you just come back to the mantra (a Hindu word meaning "mind vehicle"—as it is the vehicle that carries you away from those pesky thoughts). With TM, practitioners are given their mantra in a special ceremony and are instructed to meditate for twenty minutes, twice every day. But there are other ways to practice mantra meditation, too, and there's plenty of info online.

With mindfulness meditation, the key is to simply pay attention to your thoughts and consciously detach from them as they pass by. Practitioners of mindfulness meditation (which is rooted in Buddhist tradition) often focus on the in-and-out rhythm of the breath as a way to detach from the thoughts as they stream past like cars on a busy highway. With this analogy in mind, you can imagine that you're sitting in a comfy patio chair at the side of the road, not "minding" anything that zooms past. Just observing. *Witnessing*.

The intention with both these practices is not to *stop* the thoughts, but simply to notice them. The meditation part is not the activity itself—*it is the action of detaching from and becoming the observer of your thinking*.

To practice either of these techniques, all you need is a quiet place to sit and go inward—ideally somewhere private and safe, where you also feel comfortable to close your eyes and where you know you won't be interrupted. You can begin with just a few minutes each day and work up to longer time in meditation if it works for you. The key, my friends, is regularity. Five minutes of meditation every day is wayyyyy more effective than thirty minutes once a week. And if it doesn't feel like you "get it" right away, remember, they don't call it a "practice" for nothing. There are many other styles of meditation out there for you to try, too. The key is to find the right one for you. A bit like dating, you might have to kiss a lot of frogs before you find "the one."

For example, Centering Prayer could be a good fit if you're a Christian. Founded by Thomas Keating, an American Catholic monk, it's not meant to replace regular prayer but is a form of meditation similar to TM that uses sacred words from the Bible instead of Hindu mantras. Then there are physical practices like qigong, sketching, walking in nature, and yoga, and even repetitive exercise like jogging and swimming, which can all be "meditative" for some people. The key is to consciously use these activities to detach from your thoughts.

As it pertains to our daily lives, the real gift of meditation is that it allows us to step back and examine all of the aspects of our life. This brings perspective and clarity where we may have been too caught up in the whats and the hows and the whys to be able to see a way out. By creating a little space between your monkey mind, your changing emotions, and your deepest truths ON THE DAILY, meditation gives you the space to see with clear eyes.

Even better, over time, touching base regularly with the "you" who is so much more than your thoughts helps a soul feel increasingly at home in their body and mind. Which (and here comes the cosmic bit, which we'll discuss in more detail elsewhere) *gives the other people around you permission to feel the same.*

Underneath all the crap, we are *all* children of the Universe, and only by shutting out the external noise and coming back to silence are we able to really know and embrace this fact. If we can't experience this for ourselves, how can we expect anybody else to? Another cool thing about meditation: once you start living in a more calm, nonreactive, and emotionally stable way, everybody around you gets to reap the benefits of the calmer, less reactive you!

This is when life starts to become a whole lot more interesting. MAGIC starts to flow into your reality, and a Higher Power begins to direct your actions without you even having to ask. Overthinking things (yeah, that old energy-suck) will no longer be necessary. You will just *know* what's up, and you will feel guided to make the next right steps. Essential for anybody who is in Deep Shift, meditation is the deceptively simple practice that will deliver to you this gift.

Just Surrender Already

Okay, I know I'm making some pretty bold claims here—like telling you the answer to all your problems is to take a load off, sit still, and basically just breathe. What makes me so comfortable sharing this with you? Because I have experienced it firsthand. As stated earlier, my whole world opened up to me when I began meditating.

As you also know, I've been interested in spirituality for as long as I can remember. But nothing, and I mean *nothing*, could have prepared me for the life-altering experiences, mind-expanding perspective shifts, and world-rocking bliss that occurred for me after I learned to meditate. And as with Deep Shift itself, this is something you need to experience for yourself. It's not enough to simply read about it or listen to some yogi talking about it in a podcast.

This is why, before we go any further, I'm recommending (read: insisting) that you learn to meditate. Think about this as the crown jewel in your Shifter toolbox. Or, if you already have a practice, then it's time to deepen your daily dives into the cosmic ocean within you like your life depended on it. Because let's face it: without getting *too* dramatic, for anybody in the throes of a full-on Deep Shift, right about now it probably feels like it does!

As also discussed, it was the first time I meditated that I experienced the full onset of my first Deep Shift. My Shift began when I started spiraling after my mom died; within just *twenty minutes* of practicing Transcendental Meditation, my entire reality was transformed. I'm not saying this is a normal occurrence—I know my experience was *just a little bit* unique. But in my travels, I have met plenty people who have had similar experiences. And while I can't give you step-by-step instructions for how to experience this yourself, what I can do is share some of the insights I learned along the way.

One of the first lessons I got after learning to meditate was that *my life was no longer my own*. What I mean by this is that while my life is mine and nobody else's to be lived, it became clear to me that a force much greater than myself was pulling the strings. I also fully understood that *my* job was just to surrender to that power and let it show me the way. The day I learned to meditate, I finally understood *in my bones* what my mom had been telling me when she used to say that thing about God having way cooler plans for my life than I could ever come up with.

What we're talking about here, people, is the fabled concept of "surrender"—and it is another vital tool for anybody on the Shifter path. So what can surrender do for us, and what does this look like in practice?

Oftentimes, surrender comes as an aftereffect of hitting rock bottom in some area of your life. For example, let's say you're dealing with an addiction, a major loss, or some other kind of "kicking your ass" situation that has really brought you to your knees. You know, the kind of thing that likely led you here. The good news is, this is when *surrender* swoops in and comes to the rescue! In fact, you quitting trying to figure it out all on your own and being guided to pick up this book may well have been surrender in action!

As you know, right before I learned to meditate, I had lost my mom. She was my guru, my best friend, and my lifeline. When she passed away, my whole world went black and I felt lower than I ever had in my entire life. In fact, I didn't even know I was capable of being that depressed or of experiencing that much darkness and pain. I also shared with you that within weeks of my mom's death, I was suicidal. But as the world began closing in on me, little did I know that I was about to learn one of the biggest and most important lessons of my life: *how to surrender.*

By the time I found myself on my hands and knees sobbing uncontrollably in the shower, begging God to either help me end my life or help me live, I was no longer capable of making any decisions for myself, and so I literally had no choice but to give it up to God. I needed my Higher Power to take the wheel in a BIG WAY. And when I handed over the reins, for the first time in a very, very long time, I felt nothing. No pain, no anxiety, no grief . . . *nothing.* The respite this bought me gave me enough time to go to that life-changing dinner with my ex where I would meet the man who told me about TM.

Not that everybody has to reach as extreme of a low as I did to experience all the benefits and mind-blowing shifts in consciousness. But if you're in Deep Shift, chances are you can relate to some of what I've shared. And what

I do know is that meditation is how we unplug from the stress, the anxiety, and the distractions of the outside world, so that we can plug directly into our Higher Power. For anybody in Deep Shift, this is where the magic happens.

If my mother's death was what propelled me into Deep Shift, then learning to meditate was like finding the keys to unlocking its gifts. Now, the Shifts were coming fast and strong, and in the *best* possible way. Given that I'd been ready to literally end it all, this can only be described as an all-out miracle. Looking back, though, I can see that my Deep Shift had been a long time coming. And I'm talkin' wayyyy back.

I truly believe that everything happens for a reason (as if you didn't know this about me by now). But still, it took my mom's passing to blow up my reality and actually learn to *live* this spiritual truth. It took being brought to the edge, almost taking my life, and having no option but to admit: "I can't do this anymore. Please, someone, help me!" As intense as this sounds, I *needed all this to happen* to enter fully into the magic of Deep Shift, and to allow the Divine to do its work and overhaul my entire life as I knew it.

The moral of the story, dear Shifter, is this: accepting that you are no longer in control of your life will set you up for an incredible journey, and meditation is what will help you ride the waves while you're learning how to Shift up a gear and take ownership of your life. For this reason, daily meditation is an essential part of the program—the food that will nourish you, the fuel that will fill your spiritual tanks, and the anchor that will keep you stable when the waves get high or choppy.

To recap quickly before we move on, we use meditation to go to a place deep within us, where a profound silence allows us to listen to and embody the truth of who we are: pure, extra-virgin, A-grade *consciousness*. No stories, no projections, no bullshit. From this place, we can begin moving beyond the assumed limits of the mind and rise to meet any changes that are occurring in our life *from the inside out*. And *this* is the key to the radical personal transformation we are being invited to step into when we're in Deep Shift.

When we meditate regularly, we're able to stay calmer in hairy situations, to tap more easily into our deep creativity, and, my favorite, to not only see past illusions but set the whole veil on fire! Not least, we're also able to loosen our grip on the external outcomes we think are what will make us happy and bring us peace (outcomes that simply are no longer relevant to the cosmic trip we're on), as we give it over to a frankly way cooler universal plan.

Of course, it's ironic that learning to surrender is what puts you firmly in the driver's seat of life. But imagine that your "car" is a super-futuristic self-driving Batmobile that knows exactly how to beat the traffic and get to your destination via the most mind-blowingly beautiful scenic route.

And if this all sounds kinda trippy and far-out, I repeat: when we meditate, we are simply coming back to ourselves. Even cooler, eventually, we begin *to become* the vast, limitless silence, the pure awareness underlying all you see, think, and do. The more you meditate, the more you understand that regular dips (as in daily, in case you didn't get this memo yet) into the silent ocean of consciousness within is all that's really needed for the Shifter to thrive in this world. Let alone to navigate the wild and wavy waters of Deep Shift.

Simple Mindfulness Meditation Technique

TM is very much its own unique thing, and ideally you need to be taught it one-to-one. But committing to any daily meditation will help you navigate the waters of Deep Shift. Follow these simple steps to begin to incorporate meditation into your life:

Step 1 Find a quiet place to meditate, free of distracting noise, the sound of the TV or radio, or any other possible distractions or interruptions. (Turn your phone to silent/do not disturb mode.)

Step 2 Sit in a chair or upright on a pillow, the ground, or a bed. (If you meditate lying down, you'll probably fall asleep, defeating the purpose of meditating for expanded consciousness.)

Step 3 Close your eyes and take a minute to just be aware of your body, simply noticing whatever sensations are going on within your body.

Step 4 Gently bring your attention to your breathing. Just observe the inward and outward flow of your breath as you sit quietly. If you find you're focusing on your thoughts, gently bring your awareness back to your breath, inhaling and exhaling effortlessly.

As you continue in this simple form of meditation, you may begin noticing a slowing down of your breath, or a state of relaxation emerging. Just carry on innocently, not focusing overmuch on anything at all, returning your attention easily to the flowing in and out of your breath. I suggest, in the beginning, that you do this for a few minutes in the morning before you get engaged with your day's activities, and another few minutes at the end of your day before you start preparing for dinner. Then, when you're comfortable with this simple process of meditating, you can extend it to ten to twenty minutes per session.

CHAPTER 6

Life Is Not an Out-of-Body Experience

"Our body is precious. It is our vehicle for
awakening. Treat it with care."

Buddha

O kay. You have officially entered "the Transformation Zone," and this is going to require you to get—and *keep*—your shit together when it comes to your physical health and well-being. Things can get wild out there, and staying balanced and grounded in your body is going to be essential when it comes to keeping both feet on the ground. Which means treating your body like the miracle-working time-and-space machine that it is. Something that I learned the hard way.

I want to tell you a little story about a gal who had a fourteen-year sleep disorder; partied like a rock star; lived on espresso, adrenaline, and red wine; completely crashed and burned; and turned it all around after a twenty-minute meditation. I know this lady inside and out, because that gal is me.

It began the day my fifty-eight-year-old mom told me she had stage four breast cancer. It was a weeknight, and she'd asked me to come home for dinner. I had the day off from work and I thought, *Why not? I'd love to spend some time with Mom.* Little did I know that this particular evening would completely change the way my nervous system functioned.

After we'd hung around the kitchen for about thirty minutes, Mom poured me a glass of wine. She said, "Val, sit down. I have to talk to you about something."

My blood ran cold. I blurted out, "Oh my God! Who's dead?"

Mom laughed and told me no one was dead, but that we had to talk about her health. I could see she was being very careful with her words, in order to protect me. So I just stopped talking and looked at her, listening for all I was worth.

"I have breast cancer, Valerie, but I've got an amazing doctor at the University of Chicago and everything's going to be okay."

With tears streaming down my face, I asked, "What stage is it?"

Mom put her head down and softly said, "Stage four."

My mind and nervous system blew up. She'd basically just informed me she was a dead woman walking. I felt like someone had slammed me in the head with a bag of bricks. It was as though all my senses exploded at once, and my whole body started freaking out. My mom was my best friend, the love of my life; in that moment, my world came crashing down around me. A primal fear ripped through me, as though losing her meant I'd be alone in darkness and sadness forever. *How was I supposed to go on? Who was going to take care of me?*

It was that night that I started experiencing major-league sleep issues and insomnia became my new reality. I started having terrible nightmares and woke up every night around 3 a.m., never able to get back to sleep. During the day I felt anxious and wired, running on adrenaline, and always with my mom's diagnosis and her inevitable death at the forefront of my mind. Emotionally, I felt I was living a true hell-on-earth scenario.

I later found out that her doctor had only given her six months to live. Mom had failed to disclose that minor detail (or perhaps she chose to withhold it). Lucky for us, she *did* have an amazing oncologist who suggested she get into a trial they were conducting into a new drug that is now a common cancer treatment. That doctor's words to my mom were, "At this point you have nothing to lose." And, by the grace of God, the trial *worked*! My mom ended up living *fourteen* more years. But it wasn't an easy ride, by any means.

Over that time span, there were endless rounds of chemo, many surgeries, hospital stays, radiation treatments, and a whole lotta desperation on my part. I went to every appointment with her. Meanwhile, my brother had been in and out of psych wards for his schizophrenia since I was fifteen. It was like he was in a new Deep Shift every single day; I never knew when the other shoe was going to drop. Now I also knew that at some point I was going to lose my mom, which had me riding a roller-coaster of anxiety that was enough to completely wreck my body. Sure, I was functioning, but internally I was a mess. Side note: you cannot live with that much fear and anxiety, without getting proper sleep for fourteen years, and think you're going to come out of it without your physical and mental health taking a major beating.

As I mentioned, it was after I started meditating that my sleeping disorder literally disappeared overnight. I mean, after learning to meditate, I slept fifteen hours at a time for two weeks straight. That's what I call some serious sleep debt. But the good news is, once I started sleeping like a bear, a level of clarity and calm that I hadn't experienced in my life washed over me. This was now my reality. My new normal.

One of the first things that became crystal clear was I needed to take *much* better care of myself from that point on. And I'm here to deliver the exact same prescription to you. The thing is, when you've been down as long as I was and then you enter Deep Shift, the "honeymoon phase" can be very intoxicating—sort of like you're in a dream state, where nothing is real. It can be easy to forget to bring your human suit along for the ride when your soul is accelerating so quickly. At other times, it's more like your body can't keep up—and this is when things can get a little crazy (see the next chapter).

It can be tempting to want to escape from a physical reality that feels like it's crumbling around your ears and to avoid leaning into the more gnarly aspects of the Shift, but the whole point of this ride is NOT to emigrate to a different planet. It's to transform your life here on Earth. Simply put, this is no time to be flying away with the fairies. Your body is your anchor, and to nurture and sustain yourself during Deep Shift, and to usher in a radical transformation of consciousness that *lasts*, maintaining a healthy body, mind, and nervous system is essential. So let's go over some of what I learned the hard way, which will hopefully help you find *balance* and *grounding*, wherever you're at on the Deep Shift spectrum.

Fuel for the Ride

Let's start by looking at what you put *in* your body. As you understand by now, we Shifters are typically sensitive types, and this extends to what we eat. The thing is, food sensitivities may not actually show up until after you've entered Deep Shift. Before I had my transformation, I subsisted on a steady diet of pizza, wine, grilled cheese sandwiches, and ice cream. Y'know, the staples of the typical all-American diet. But when all your senses become heightened, and you opt in to feeling ALL your feelings, it's not unusual to become uber-sensitive to the way different foods make you feel. And wouldn't you know, it turns out my standard diet was not serving me at all.

Nowadays, I look at food as fuel. Don't get me wrong, I LOVE food. I have just become much pickier when it comes to what types of food I eat. And I am not alone. In my experience, dinner is never the same again for anyone who finds themself in Deep Shift as it's no longer possible to ignore the fact that we are *literally* what we eat. It's like your body no longer allows for anything less than *exactly what it needs* to thrive.

For example (surprise), I started feeling more sensitive to food and booze right after I learned to meditate. I would eat something that wasn't right for me—something I had been eating just fine for years—and I would literally pass out. Let's say I ate a couple slices of greasy pizza. About ten minutes after I would finish my meal, I would have to lie down and go to sleep. I'm talking, game over for the rest of the day. Say *what?!* After the twentieth time this happened to me (clearly, I'm not a quick learner), I began to ask myself, *What the hell is happening? Am I allergic to (insert food item)?* Before my Deep Shift, I could, and would, eat anything. And I mean *anything*. Had my constitution really changed so much that a bowl of ice cream or a grilled cheese sandwich could take me down? The answer was, "Yup, it sure did."

So I took my butt down to the best functional medicine doctor I could find, looking for evidence to determine exactly what was going on. She suggested I keep a food diary and mark down the times I ate, what I ate, and how I felt before and after I ate. Holy shit, was *this* eye-opening! From a simple review of my diary entries, it was clear as day that there were certain foods I just could not stomach. Literally.

My functional medicine doc also had me tested for food allergies and food sensitivities. I needed some cold hard facts if I was going to give up my favorite foods, something I knew was *not* going to come easy. And so off I went to get tested, which we both hoped would identify more clearly what was really going on. Within days, I had my answers. My blood work showed I had sensitivities to dairy, gluten (the worst for me), peanuts, and a whole laundry list of other things I had been eating on the regular. My doc also told me I should ditch sugar because it would just make my energy levels crash. Staring at my test results, I wondered if I would ever enjoy food again!

It's no fun eating and then feeling like crap, but it's also not fun giving up a whole bountiful buffet of the foods you love. Especially if (like most of us) you eat for pleasure as much as sustenance. I had to make a decision. My radical transformation and expansion into a magical new consciousness . . . or the curly fries? Ultimately, I chose my Deep Shift.

As for *why* this happens? The only way I can describe it is that you can no longer get away with things you once did. Your body will force you to change, which is another way the Universe shows us that we are not in control. We don't get to pick and choose what works for us and what doesn't. Our body is now making the rules, and it's on us Shifters to keep up and adjust.

Over time, I made my new dietary regime work by becoming a better cook. To the point that I actually began to *enjoy* cooking at home. I also noticed I could literally feel the energy in the foods when I was choosing what to buy at the grocery store, and shopping itself became an exercise in consciousness. Holding each vegetable in my hands, I would ask, "Which will be best for me?" This practice made me feel connected to my food, connected to my body, and even more connected to the earth.

And wouldn't you know, without me even realizing it, I had become a *conscious eater*. Now there's not a day that goes by when I'm not grateful for this transition. I still occasionally indulge, but I now cook fabulous meals at home and use the food I eat as a grounding tool in and of itself. Which means, dear Shifter, that I encourage you too to lean into and embrace the old adage: "Food is thy medicine." Instead of thinking of any dietary changes you know you need to make as "giving up" your favorite foods, this means making eating into an incredible, transformative adventure in and of itself.

Food Diary for Deep Shifters

If you're looking to get clarity on what food will best serve you during Deep Shift, I highly recommend the food diary exercise my doctor had me do. Ideally, it's done over the course of two months, but start with just a week. Keep a journal, or write in the notes section on your phone and list everything you eat in a day, and then follow this with some notes on how you feel after. You can also include details of WHERE you are eating and with WHO—as the environment can also impact our ability to properly digest our food. Over time, this will help you gain clarity around how to get the most nourishment and enjoyment out of the food you eat.

The Hard Stuff

Okay, we can't discuss food without talking about caffeine and alcohol— two hardcore *drugs*, people, that most of us use on a regular basis without even thinking about it. Now, many people won't need to give up or cut back on these things in order to feel aligned and grounded in their body, but for some, coffee and alcohol are big coping mechanisms for facing emotions and hard truths. For example: coffee. We live in a caffeine-addicted world with a Starbucks on every corner. But for many a Shifter, caffeine makes us feel loopy.

Did I mention I had an issue with sleep? Well, guess what wasn't doing me any favors in that department. For me, realizing I would have to give up coffee was another hard pill to swallow. I was a lady who LOVED her double espresso. No cream or sugar required—I preferred mainlining it straight into my veins and taking off like a rocket. But oh my, how times have changed. These days, even the tiny hint of caffeine that's in decaf coffee can spin me off into La-La Land (with a side of anxiety). Fortunately, I've found an alternative I can live with and have actually come to love: dandelion tea (especially the brand Dandy Tea) with steamed oat milk and a sprinkle of cinnamon. I *swear* it tastes just like the real thing without the gnarly side effects.

And it's the same with booze. Alcohol is something most of us use to kick back and relax, including yours truly back in the day. In fact, I believe that many a-Shifter uses alcohol to take the edge off their heightened sensitivity—it's hard work feeling everything all the time! Being this sensitive in an insensitive world can be totally overwhelming, and numbing our senses with alcohol often seems like the easy route in the moment. A way to just turn it all off.

But clearly, drinking alcohol to sooth your sensitive nature isn't the answer. Not only are we more likely to become addicted to alcohol when we use it as a coping mechanism, but being more sensitive means we're ALSO more sensitive to the toxins in booze, and more likely to experience negative side effects. This effect will only be heightened while you're in Deep Shift. And the truth is, alcohol is just keeping you from your true self. If you're boozing all the time, you're just prolonging the process of awakening. When you're in Deep Shift, you are being forced to transform. To really look at your shit and transmute it. Alcohol doesn't help this process; in fact, it only makes things more confusing.

In my case, I couldn't drink AT ALL for a full year after I learned to meditate and entered fully into my Deep Shift. Even one sip of alcohol would make me feel very VERY WEIRD. Now that things have calmed down and I'm out the other side of the Shift, I can have a glass or two—but any more and I really feel it. But then, I also feel naturally high on life, so I don't even "need" booze like I used to!

The wild thing is, you may find yourself tempted to use Deep Shift to rationalize or justify your continued use of alcohol (or other drugs, even). When the Shift is hitting the fan, common wisdom is to reach for a drink or a smoke to help us chill the F out. But let's face it: no one has ever gotten more *balanced* and *grounded* through imbibing booze and drugs.

Remember, the goal is to stay IN YOUR BODY, and both caffeine and alcohol have the opposite effect. Worse, both exacerbate anxiety, and the idea here is to stay as calm as possible so we can face the challenges of the Shift head-on and simultaneously sit back and just trust the process. I know that giving up booze is a big deal for most people—it's so ingrained in our society to drink! If this feels particularly daunting to you, you have literally nothing to lose (given that it's free!) by checking out an AA meeting. There is NO SHAME in getting extra help with this, and I've already told you how much I swear by the twelve-step programs (and again, THEY'RE FREE).

But I'm also not here to preach—as with everything about being in Deep Shift, this is about being honest about what works for you! What I will say is that you and your well-being *have to* come first. You are officially in superhuman bootcamp, and taking a break from booze is such a small sacrifice when you think about the big picture. Any time the going gets tough, the answer is not to check out; it's time to choose whatever helps you stay *with* whatever is coming up for you. Trust me: on the other side you will feel INVINCIBLE.

Eat, Move, Sweat

Okay, so on to the next *staying-calm-while-you're-being-rocked-by-the-waves-of-massive-change* tip: food itself can also be used to ward off the scary monster we know as anxiety. Scientists at Harvard University and other major research centers have helped identify a number of foods that actually trigger the release of neurotransmitters like serotonin and dopamine, giving us that "feel good" response we all want (and that we're looking for any time we reach for mood-enhancing substances). Here are some of the basics of an anti-stress diet:

- Foods that are naturally rich in magnesium have been found to have calming effects. These include leafy greens, such as spinach and Swiss chard, legumes, nuts (especially Brazil nuts), seeds, and whole grains.

- Foods rich in omega-3 fatty acids are also good for reducing anxiety and depression. If you eat fish, stock up on wild Alaskan salmon. For vegetarians and vegans, sources include walnuts, flaxseeds, chia seeds, hemp seeds, edamame, and seaweed. (Since these are not the easiest to incorporate in your diet, you may want to consider taking a quality supplement.)

- Zinc has been found to lower anxiety, hence the recommendation to include foods like cashews and (for meat-eaters) liver, beef, oysters, and egg yolks in your diet.

- Probiotic-rich foods, such as kefir, sauerkraut/kimchi, and pickles, as well as foods rich in B-vitamins—almonds and avocados—have been shown to have calming effects.

But diet is just one piece of the anti-anxiety puzzle. After you've taken the dive into Deep Shift, *moving your body* isn't a suggestion—it's a *must*. Ugh. I can almost hear you groan! We've been trained to think of exercise as a chore (no pain, no gain!), but rather than a punishment, I'm talking about making daily movement a practice to help keep the juju flowing.

As opposed to "how many calories will this burn" or "how toned will this get me" (more yucky thinking about exercise that's rooted in punishing or trying to control our bodies), the key thing to ask when picking something that will carry you through Deep Shift is: "*Will this move the energy around my body?*" Yoga, dance, and aerobics are all great for this, but if I can encourage you to take up one form of exercise above all others, it's walking (ideally in nature and fast enough to break a sweat). It's going to be a game changer.

Think about it: when we're anxious, we "pace." Our body *wants* us to walk off the anxiety. And there is an evolutionary explanation for why this is. In humans, the problem-solving part of our brains (the frontal lobe) developed at the same time as we evolved to walk upright on two legs. As such, "figuring shit out" and walking go hand-in-hand. I know people who have their best ideas speed-walking around the block, but more often than not, "figuring shit out" means simply letting go and letting God.

Which is why it helps to walk in nature. When we come face-to-face with the Deep Shift, it's like the energy in our bodies accelerates. As noted, this can feel destabilizing, especially if we don't have anywhere for the energy to go. Unused energy just keeps getting recycled in our bodies as *anxiety*. Nature is designed (yes, by God) to receive our excess energy and put it back into the ground—a.k.a. *grounding*. And this, dear Shifter, is why walking in nature (or at least outdoors) can literally help to keep you sane. If you don't have access to the nature of suburbs, woods, and so on, try walking around your block a few times and just breathing in the air. Or maybe there's a park you can take a subway or bus to. Being outside is the main priority.

If you can get to a forest to do your walking, even if it's a special trip you make once or twice a year, then this will supercharge your walking-movement practice. In Japan, walking among the trees is called "forest bathing"—and scientists have proven that it has real health benefits, including lowered blood pressure and lower scores for depression, fatigue, anxiety, and confusion. This is some good shit, people!

When you're in Deep Shift, what's equally important is to actually break a sweat, every damned day. Why? Getting your body to the point that your heart is beating, toxins are being purged, and the oxygen is flowing *shows* that things are moving.

I met a man, a fellow Shifter, and we had a long discussion about this very topic. He'd been on a long meditation course and told me how he had "pierced the veil" mid-course. Deep Shift had fallen upon him, and he intuitively knew he had to *move* the energy inside of his body. And so this fellow decided the best thing he could do was get a construction job, in the heat of summer, so he could make physical labor and sweating his tail off part of his daily livelihood. Now *that*, my friends, was a wizard-level Shifter move.

I'm not saying you have to do something as radical as this (unless you feel called to—which I am definitely not ruling out for you at this point!). But the prescription is pretty simple: when it comes to staying in your body and getting grounded so the Shifter anxiety doesn't get the better of you, the words to live by are *eat, move, sweat.* This means choosing the food that will truly fuel you, getting off your butt, and getting the energy (and the anxiety) moving.

And Don't Forget to Breathe!

Okay, people, breathing. It may be one of the most important things you ever learn to do. I can hear you talking back at me right now: "Duh, I know how to *breathe*, Val." But I bet you a gluten-free almond-flour cookie you're not doing it properly, and especially not when you're under stress or feeling anxious—otherwise known as having the world as you know it turned on its head in every which way possible because you're in Deep Shift.

First of all, you want to train yourself to breathe through your nose as much as possible. Why is this, and what the heck does it have to do with staying balanced and grounded while you're in Deep Shift? It turns out that nitric oxide greatly increases and circulates in your blood when you breathe through your nose. You want this to happen, because when you have more nitric oxide in your bloodstream you get a boatload of benefits. Check out this list:

- Lowered blood pressure

- Improved heart function

- Stronger immune system

- Better brain health

- More energy

- And my personal favorite, decreased chance of developing anxiety and depression

The proof is in the pudding. Breathing properly is a major contributor to your well-being and a surefire way to keep you as cool as a cucumber. But when we think about breathing, we figure it's just something our bodies do on autopilot, right? Um, wrong. What most of us never learned in school, at church, or from our parents, is that breathing is an actual, bona fide superpower. I first found out about this after reading a book that was recommended to me by a friend (a retired medical doctor), *Breath: The New Science of a Lost Art*, by James Nestor.

In my spiritual studies, I had picked up that many yogic masters and sages throughout the ages have advocated the use of breath control as a meditation in itself, or to enhance one's daily practice of meditation. Once I learned pranayama (an East Asian form of meditative breath control), I had experienced all sorts of benefits myself. But Nestor's book goes deep into the details of just how powerful learning and practicing the art of breathing can be!

The bottom line is this: through our breath we have the ability to control our psychology and, therefore, the way we feel. Scientific studies have shown that the way we breathe influences our nervous system, hormones, blood pressure, digestion, and heart rate. Taking all these benefits as a whole, breathing can literally extend your life span and greatly improve the quality of your life. Pretty impressive for something we all do naturally all day long, and which we usually pay little or no attention to!

So, what is the proper way to breathe? Let's break it down:

1. Breathe through your nose (you got this one, right?). Make sure your mouth is closed and your tongue is touching the top of your mouth. It sounds easy, but if you really pay attention, you will see that you breathe through your mouth more than you know, especially when you're distracted or zoned out.

2. Take a minute to breathe "consciously" throughout the day. Every time you remember to check in, take a full, deep breath into your chest. Also try to notice any time you are unconsciously holding your breath.

3. Count it out. The 4-7-8 technique is my personal favorite for this. Based on an ancient Hatha yoga technique (i.e., one of the forms of pranayama), you inhale for four seconds, hold your breath for seven seconds and then exhale for eight seconds. Easy-peasy!

We've only scratched the surface on ways to keep grounded, balanced, and as calm as a millpond through breath, but I'll be sprinkling more ideas in the chapters to come. For now, make it your daily mission to keep your feet on the ground and your head in the sky, the better to anchor yourself in the transformational process of your Deep Shift.

CHAPTER 7

Help, I'm Having a Spiritual Emergency

*"There can be no rebirth without a dark night of the soul,
a total annihilation of all that you believed
and thought that you were."*

Inayat Khan

a s we've established, when you're in Deep Shift, MAJOR change is the only certainty. *Everything* is up for grabs, and with any full-tilt transformation there can be serious bumps in the road. It ain't always pretty and, I'm not gonna lie, sometimes it can get scary as hell. Enter the phenomenon known as a Spiritual Emergency. Now, my job is not to freak you out but to point out the possible potholes in advance. That way, if shit *does* go south, you'll be better prepared to stay afloat if and when things start spinning out of control.

Note my use of the word "if." In reality, only a teeeeeeeny percentage of Deep Shifters will experience the kind of, um, event I am about to describe to you. But I'm including it here as both a reference point for if things *do* start to go wonky and a cautionary tale for you to pump the breaks any time the Shift starts getting uncomfortably weird.

So far, all you've heard about my Deep Shift is how miraculous life became for me after I learned to meditate and began to transform every aspect of my world. But there was one major "happening" along the way that almost completely derailed me. Before I get into the details of what went down, when I talk about a Spiritual Emergency, I mean what Christians refer to as the Dark Night of the Soul. It can take the form of a physical, mental, and/or spiritual breakdown, and it can be fucking horrifying.

Yes, this is something I experienced myself—and before you get too freaked out, check it: I am totally here to tell the tale! While a Spiritual Emergency can feel like the end of times while you're in the thick of it, it is not the same as an actual psychotic break, which I also have firsthand experience of thanks to my brother's schizophrenia. I'll be sharing how to spot the difference here, as well as everything I learned about how to survive and recover from a hell-on-wheels Spiritual Emergency and come out the other side stronger than ever. I have since done a ton of research on the subject, and in fact there is a whole library of books on the subject—which, if nothing else, proves that if you do find yourself in this situation, you are definitely not the first nor will you be the last.

I would also like to add that I am not a doctor, a counselor, or a therapist. Yes, I have a master's degree in transpersonal psychology, but I can't diagnose you or give you a guaranteed prescription that will work for you. I can only share what happened to me and what has helped me along the way. In my case, as with all the changes that my Deep Shift brought on, my Spiritual Emergency came on fast and strong. All I could do was hold on for dear life and pray my head wouldn't spin off my goddamned body! Assuming you are suitably intrigued, here's how shit went down.

Somebody Call Spiritual 911

In 2014, three years after I first learned to meditate, I found myself sitting in a room with twenty-four other women quietly meditating, while praying—no, *begging*—for God to spare my life. In the space of seconds, I went from chilling and meditating with everybody else to feeling like I was either going to have a heart attack or explode. There was so much energy coursing through my body, it was like I'd plugged myself into a wall and my head was about to blow off my body. But while I sat there, soaking with sweat, frozen on the spot in my own personal hell, from the outside, nobody would have been able to tell what was happening to me.

What propelled me to feel that way? As you know, soon after I learned to meditate, I felt like I had been handed a new set of kaleidoscope eyes through which to see the world. A couple of weeks into my new spiritual practice, I knew there was no turning back. I was such an enthusiastic student, in fact, that my meditation teacher invited me to visit various corporations with her and talk about the benefits of meditation. Over the next year, I watched hundreds of people learn to meditate. One by one, I saw their eyes light up, too. And so it was that I decided to dedicate my life to helping others find their way in the unchartered waters of awakening (hi!). It was here, in the realm of expanding consciousness, that I had found my destiny.

As time went on, I also found I wanted to deepen my own meditation practice. Since meditation had already given me so much, I felt a strong desire to explore further. And so when the opportunity came up to attend the TM-Sidhi Program, an advanced meditation course that's taught over five weeks in Fairfield, Iowa, where I was living at the time, I jumped on it.

The course was only held a couple of times a year, and the next time enrollment came around I cleared my schedule and started gearing up for this new adventure. I didn't read about it on the internet or allow anyone to tell me about what happens in the course; I wanted to walk into it completely free from any preconceptions. That's how I like to roll when it comes to spiritual teachings—preferring not to let anybody else's notions about how it should all shake out influence my experience. The only thing I knew about the TM-Sidhi Program was that the course was super-intense. But as a dedicated meditator, I knew I would completely connect with it.

The first three weeks of the course consisted of attending class for two to three hours a day, during which we learned a variety of advanced meditation techniques. No problem. I felt really good—amazing, actually. When I'd return home after each class, colors were brighter, my energy levels were off the charts, and my mind was clear as a bell. I was digging it. Then we began the two-week in-residence segment of the program. Now we were meditating for most of the day, and when we weren't immersed in silence we were engaging in discussions about consciousness, doing lots of walking, and eating vegetarian food.

First week, same thing. I felt extra groovy and described a sense of being "carried through life" to the course leaders. I told them how I felt as if I was connected to everything, the very same feeling as when I first started meditating. I would float out of my sessions in a state of ecstasy that lasted for hours. As if I was in God and God was in me. Now, this feeling was intensified, but it was a state that felt very familiar to me, so I just went with it. Then the final week rolled around, and we were taught the last part of the new, three-part meditation that we'd been practicing.

As with each part of the practice, each new lesson is passed from teacher to student in a systematic and traditional way. This involves a short ceremony giving thanks to the previous teachers of the TM tradition, and then the simple instruction is passed on to the student. Easy-breezy. I've seen it a hundred times, and it's as familiar to me as eating an apple. Well, not this time. As the ceremony began, for some reason my heart started racing. The meditation teacher gave all of us the instructions. On the surface, it was simple—however, inside my mind and body, well, that was quite a different story.

I started to meditate with everybody else, just like I'd done literally hundreds of times before. But as I gently began to incorporate my new instruction, it was as if a door inside my soul got ripped right off the hinges, and all the energy from the entire Universe hit me like a hurricane! Nothing in the external world had moved an inch, but on the inside I felt as if twenty hits of acid had entered my bloodstream all at once and at the same time as I plugged myself into an electrical socket. I've had plenty of panic attacks in my time, but this was different; I felt like I was literally going to die *and* go insane in the same moment.

While everyone else in the room quietly continued meditating, I began to pray like I've never prayed before. Tears started to fall from my eyes as I begged for God to let me live. I would have jumped up and sprinted out of the building, but I was frozen, unable to move, think, or speak. I was a Popsicle suspended in time with high-voltage electricity streaming through my veins. As the clock ticked on the wall, twenty minutes felt like ten lifetimes. My new mantra at this point was, "God, please let me live . . . God, please save me!"

When it was all over, I told my teacher what had happened. I stood in front of her with tears streaming down my face, and she looked stunned. Clearly, she was not used to this type of extreme reaction from her students;

just a day earlier, I'd been telling her how I felt like I was walking on sunshine. And little did I know, this was only the beginning of my Spiritual Emergency. I would not be able to meditate, eat, sleep, or function properly for *days* following the incident. Recovering fully from this experience over the following months and years became an important part of my Deep Shift.

I ran to the bathroom down the hall and threw up everywhere, kind of like that girl in *The Exorcist*. And the waves of mania just kept hitting me, hour after hour. That night, I tried to sleep, but I was too scared to close my eyes. For four straight days, I felt like I was clinging to the Jaws of Life. I began to question if I would ever feel "normal" again. Had I broken my brain?

I knew it was common enough for people to occasionally have "abnormal" reactions when meditating for long periods of time. I'd heard stories about people releasing tons of stress and kind of flipping out. But nothing like this had ever happened to anyone I knew. I also knew that when stress starts to leave your body, it can come out in extreme ways, causing everything from breakouts to extreme anxiety and confusion. But if this was what was going on, then the sheer level of disturbance I was experiencing was off the charts.

Despite the panic, the vomiting, and the overall insanity, I kept showing up to class, even though I wasn't participating fully. It took every inch of courage I had just to close my eyes. I know, I'm a wild woman, right? I was the most scared I have ever been in my life, but somewhere inside of me my intuition kept saying, "You are going to make it and you're going to be stronger than ever. This is happening for a reason. Just let go. Surrender."

Now, the instructors were well aware that something was up, but they didn't seem to know what to do with me. By day four, I was told if I didn't continue with the program in some way, shape, or form, I would have to be sent home (which would mean I'd be the only one out of fifty people not to finish). At that point the warrior in me emerged, and after some negotiating on my part I told them, "If you can slow this train down for me, I will see it through."

And so that's what they did. I was instructed to meditate for only thirty minutes a day (instead of the four to six hours that everybody else was doing), and a teacher would sit with me while I practiced the new program. It took every bit of courage for me to again try out the one particularly powerful meditation that had thrown me for such a loop. Once I was settled in between two teachers, and separated from the other people in the room, I was able to go there—but only after asking God and my mom to protect me. And then—just like the time I said yes to going skydiving with my friend—I closed my eyes and stepped over the edge of reality and into another dimension.

What came next blew my mind. I had the *opposite* experience of my previous meditation. This time, instead of diving into the depths of hell, I shot up into a "field" I can only believe was heaven. I had never entered this space before, but it was filled with everything and nothing at the same time. I was also completely, fully aware in this new dimension . . . and with my inner, kaleidoscope eyes wide open, I took it all in.

Afterward, my teachers told me my head had been facing straight up in the air, locked in place, toward the ceiling. This made sense to me, because it felt like I'd shot up through my head and "fallen upward" right into this new world. When they asked me what I'd experienced, I looked at them and simply said, "I think I just went to the place we end up when we die." But how was this possible? Had I had a near-death experience . . . without actually coming close to death? I mean, was I literally living in the Twilight Zone? Actually no, what I have come to believe is that I was actually experiencing an *extreme* form of Deep Shift.

Coming Back Down

After the smoke cleared and I began to get a grip on reality and drift back down to earth, I realized it was my *ego* that was dying on that course. The feeling of panic and horror I had experienced was the remaining claws of my small self clinging on, like a mad dog holding tightly to a bone that's already been picked dry. Like everything else in my spiritual life, my ego death came on fast and furious—with the feelings of psychic terror continuing to wash though me for weeks after the course. To the extent that I began to question if I would ever feel "normal" again.

That's when I reached out to an old contact who had taken the same course. When I explained what had happened, he told me, "You crossed over, Val—it's time to go pro." It was a reference to what was also his favorite

Hunter S. Thompson quote. I knew he was telling me that I would have to find a way to be stronger than this. He was also a recovered addict; if anybody knew the meaning of perseverance in the face of adversity it was him, and his faith in me gave me hope that I would be able to get myself out the other side.

But even though I had never experienced anything this crazy in my life, at no point did I truly fear for my life or my sanity. I had witnessed my brother's psychotic break firsthand, and while there were some similarities in what I had experienced, the key difference was that my episode was clearly triggered by the meditation course. With him, the schizophrenia had descended from nowhere—and while I'd been hyper-aware of what was happening to me, he'd been completely blind to the fact that anything was wrong. All along, part of me knew that I was in the throes of the awakening process and that I would make it out eventually. Sadly, for my brother, it was like a switch had been permanently flicked to another channel in his brain.

Mental illness is no joke, and if at any point you or anybody you know is concerned that things have gone too far, then it's important to seek professional help; I've included some more pointers on this below. As for recovery from a Spiritual Emergency, in my case, despite weeks of confusion, panic, and soul-searching that followed my experience on the TM retreat, I can finally say, "Yes, it was worth it."

Scary as it was at the time, what I discovered "on the other side" is a whole *other* level of clarity, freedom, and knowing that I never even knew existed. And yes, once again I had to go to hell and back to get there. It must be something in my karma. I would not wish what I went through on my worst enemy. But that's just how it happened for me.

As I mentioned, I've since done a lot of reading on "happenings" like mine. The upshot? A spiritual awakening can often be precipitated by a severe emotional or spiritual crisis—the kind of life event that triggers Deep Shift in the first place. And while a true Spiritual Emergency is not that common, it can show up at different levels of intensity. The fact is, Deep Shift will stir up all kinds of shit to be processed, and depending on a number of factors (everything from environment to stress levels and a person's basic personality), this can be intense. If the reaction this triggered in me was off the charts, then it's because I was engaging in some pretty extreme behavior at the time. I mean, it's not exactly normal to meditate for up to eight hours a day! You know me well enough by now to know that I'm a gal who goes all in. In some ways, I believe I was *seeking out* what happened to me—in order to go even deeper in my Shift.

As for why this happens, my sense is that sometimes we hit a roadblock in our transformation process, and we need something to catapult us to a higher level. As if God steps in to help us get to a level of awakening we might not reach on our own. And I guess that week in Fairfield, God knew I needed another boost. After all, this was the second time in my life I'd been cracked wide open by meditation and then shoved toward a higher state of consciousness. (I mean, twice? *Really?!*) What I learned in this experience, yet again, is that once you're on your knees, the only place left to go is up. In my case, right up into the heavens.

In the Quran, the Prophet Muhammad said, "Die before you die." Without a shadow of a doubt, I can say, "Amen, brother!" to that statement. It's a sad fact of the human condition that we often get stuck in a case of mistaken identity. What Muhammad was referring to was that the "false self" (or ego—as conditioned by our parents, society, politics, etc.) has to die before we can live as our *true* self. This is essentially what's happening when we're in Deep Shift—and sometimes, a Spiritual Emergency of sorts is just a part of this process.

(Spiritual) Emergency on Planet Earth

Okay, by now you're probably asking: "So what should *I* do if I completely go off the rails, and Deep Shift starts seriously kicking my ass?" To conclude here, I'm going to share my step-by-step guide to surviving a Spiritual Emergency, based on what I've learned from my personal experience as well as all of my studies, along with conversation with friends, clients, and other people who have had similar experiences.

Step One: Recognize what's happening and tell somebody else about it.
Signs that you may be having a Spiritual Emergency include feeling like there is too much energy in your body, or like there is electricity in your head; feeling

overwhelmed; having too many thoughts; and being hyper-intuitive and sensitive. It's likely that you will never have felt like this before in your life. Less like a panic attack, it can feel more like literally being possessed. In my case, I also felt like I was nowhere *near* my body. And if somebody doesn't believe you when you describe what you're experiencing, then find somebody who does. I found a teacher at the TM center who got it, and then I connected with other mentors I'd met on my meditation journey to help me figure things out. In the United States, you can go to spiritualemergence.org for a list of crisis hotlines where you can speak to somebody right away.

Step Two: STOP ENGAGING WITH YOUR SPIRITUAL PRACTICES. Or at least seriously scale back.
When you start spinning out of control, it's a straight-up sign you need to pump the brakes. MORE meditation, MORE chanting, and MORE sound baths are not, let me repeat, NOT going to help your cause. You need to stop, drop all the bells and whistles, pull your head out of the clouds, and make like a sturdy oak tree—roots and feet firmly on the ground.

Step Three: Get back in your body.
Having a Spiritual Emergency is a sign that you've journeyed too far off into the clouds, and it's vital that you get back into your human suit ASAP. The suggestions in the previous chapter will help with this—especially the instruction to move your body! And I mean, a lot. Remember the man I told you about who grounded himself after being on a long meditation course by getting a job in construction? He basically told me, without telling me, that he had experienced a Spiritual Emergency. Doing construction work was the literal opposite of sitting and meditating all day—which was just what he needed to back off the intensity.

One of the telltale signs of a Spiritual Emergency is feeling like there's a huge amount of energy coursing through your veins—which means you need to move it up and out. The way to do it is through physical movement; this means exercise, and a whole lot of it. Swim, walk in nature (my personal favorite, as you know), jump rope, chase your dog around town, ride a bike, put on some music and shake your body. I don't care what you do, just don't sit there and let the energy get the best of you. Move it so you don't lose it.

Step Four: Maybe eat some meat.

Now, I know this is going to sound strange, but after I experienced my own Spiritual Emergency, some old-school professional meditators told me to smoke a cigar and eat a steak. This sounds pretty gross given what we know about a healthy diet today—but it was the advice *they* were given when shit got cray on their long meditation courses, including the infamous one the Beatles took in India with Maharishi Mahesh Yogi.

Having been a pescatarian since I was fifteen and a nonsmoker, this advice was pretty shocking. And while I didn't start slamming New York strip steaks, I *did* start eating some chicken and turkey. My intuition told me that some animal protein would help bring me back to Planet Earth. If you are a committed vegetarian or vegan, it might be worth investigating B-12 shots and iron supplements, as a deficiency in either (which we get from animal protein) can lead to feelings of overwhelm and anxiety that are NOT going to help you at this point.

Step Five: Talk it out.

As discussed, having somebody on your team to turn to when the Shift really hits the fan is essential. This could be a friend or family member, a mentor, or somebody you have connected with in an online support group. If you can afford it, getting yourself a good therapist to hold your hand during Deep Shift is a really great idea—especially if you start veering into Spiritual Emergency territory. Ideally, whoever you find to talk things out with should understand the concept of spiritual transformation. Keywords to look for when choosing a therapist (if this is an option for you) are transpersonal (spiritual) psychotherapist and Jungian therapist. These peeps will understand the ways of the Shifter and be able to hold your hand during the wildest of the storms.

In my case, when I shared my "episode" with my therapist, she helped me understand that the experience had basically brought *all* my past trauma about my brother's illness and my mom's death to the surface at once—and that rather than shove all this back down, now I would need to work through it all piece by piece. Only then did I realize how much I had squashed down inside me over the years; honestly, it was only going to be a matter of time before it all erupted.

Step Six: Two words. Energy work.

There are many forms of energy work, which essentially describes any practice or modality that can be used to balance the energetic systems in the body. Working out and talking it out are all well and good, but sometimes—for where things have gotten really sticky—you need something to get to places other therapies cannot reach.

Emotional Freedom Technique (EFT), a.k.a. "tapping," is a super-accessible form of energy work that you can perform on yourself. It basically involves gently tapping various energy points on your body (typically on the head, face, and upper torso) to help move stuck energy along. Nick Ortner is a leading expert on EFT, and he has numerous YouTube videos to guide you if you want to try it for yourself.

If you can afford it, then it could also be worth finding an energy worker to work with one-to-one. I was lucky enough to find an incredible guy in Santa Fe, and for two years I would take the trip to see him every other month so he could help me process the blockages in my system that were preventing the Shifter energy from moving through me. In my case, this was the energetic residue of the traumas I was working through with my therapist—as if the talk therapy and the energy work were working hand-in-hand.

Now, when it comes to energy work it is extremely important to find somebody you feel safe with and who understands what you're going through. In fact, don't stop looking till you find this person. Chemistry and trust are EVERYTHING when it comes to energy work, and if you get even a hint of a bad or off-putting feeling about a practitioner, he or she is not your person. Trust your intuition and ask for personal recommendations. I found my Santa Fe energy worker through a trustworthy friend of a friend.

Step Seven: Finally, read up about this phenomenon and get yourself informed.

Here are my top hits:

> *In Case of Spiritual Emergency: Moving Successfully Through Your Awakening,* by Catherine G. Lucas
>
> *The Stormy Search for the Self,* by Christina Grof
>
> *Spiritual Emergency: When Personal Transformation Becomes Crisis,* by Stanislav Grof
>
> *The Call of Spiritual Emergency: From Personal Crisis to Personal Transformation,* by Emma Bragdon

Reading these books made me feel less alone. Now I knew for sure that this Spiritual Emergency thing wasn't just mumbo jumbo. The stories the authors described reflected my story—and seeing myself in their words is what helped me more than anything, along with the insights they shared about how to navigate this complex situation. This is what I am hoping to do here: empower you with information, so that if and when the waters get choppy, you'll understand where the intensity is coming from. Knowledge is power. Always.

One final note: Getting through to the other side of a Spiritual Emergency—into the awakened arms of your true self—is always going to be your own personal journey. Nobody else will experience it quite the same way you do, and so rather than looking outside yourself for a quick fix (yep, like we've typically been conditioned to do!) it is vital to get the support you need to be able to trust yourself and your process.

And I repeat: if you feel like you're having an *actual* breakdown (or even coming close), get professional help, ASAP. Literally dial 911. Mental illness is majorly stigmatized, but there is zero shame in raising your hand when the going gets truly weird. There is nothing "wrong with you" if you are feeling unstable or out of control, and there are plenty of ways to get help. For now, let me leave you with this: once you buy the ticket and take the ride inward, you never know what will come up. It's time to hold on to your hats, brothers and sisters, because smashing your ego to reveal your true self is truly the ride of a lifetime.

part three

Meanwhile, Back in
the Real World . . .

CHAPTER 8

No Going Back Now . . . and Why Would You Want To?

"Better things are ahead. They are greater
than what we leave behind."

C. S. Lewis

Can I please get a big exhale? If you are reading this in real time with your transformational process, chances are that by now you feel like you've been through hell and back again. The Deep Shift washing machine has scrubbed you clean. First you got thrown in the tub, then you got swirled all around and upside down, and eventually came the spin cycle. Holy crap, is this a wild ride! But here we are. You're still in one piece. You didn't break. In fact, you may now be stronger than ever.

Not too long ago, you were probably wondering how you were going to get out of bed in the morning and face the day. Now, however, you're in a different space. The future is bright, anything is possible, and you're ready to take on your next adventure. You feel more solid inside. You Know things (yes, with a capital *K*) and you also know that you can handle whatever Life puts in front of you (yes, with a capital *L*!).

That is power, my friends. Chances are, being in Deep Shift has found you feeling beaten down, overwhelmed, and confused, and has hit you with more challenges than you thought were possible. But with your strength, your perseverance, and your willingness to go with the process (not to mention a boatload of support from the Cosmos), you have broken on through to the other side. This makes you a Super Shifter. A spiritual warrior. Basically, you are kind of a rock star, and you know it.

So now what? What are you going to do with this newfound Deep Shifter status? I'm sorry to be the one to break it to you, but you ain't going back to that old life of yours. Those days are oh-va. Never to be seen again. And you know what? It simply doesn't matter. At this point, you may be keenly aware that the old you was just one iteration of the infinite child of the Cosmos that you were born to be. That it's time to embark on a new chapter in your odyssey. This could bring new friends, possibly a new career, maybe even a new home—and most definitely some new ideas about what makes life meaningful to you.

So, when do you know what to let go of and what to bring with you for the ride? Let's start with the big stuff. The top three hits. Your friendships, your j-o-b, and your home base.

When it comes to your friendships, you are likely gonna find yourself running with a whole new crew. I'm not saying you need to ditch your old posse. Sure, if you find you feel crappy around someone or you realize they're an energy vampire, then, of course, it's time to quickly walk away in the opposite direction. But the fact is, you are (truly) a different person now. You have been equipped with an inner guidance mechanism that's plugged directly into the Universe—and that may well mean you now have completely different needs from your old circle of friends. In addition, now that you've stepped fully into your Shifter calling, the transformation will be ongoing—a path that calls for a group of humans who feed your soul, who support you no matter what, and who feel like long-lost members of your spiritual family. And you know the coolest part? Since you don't have to ditch your old buddies, now you get to have double the friends!

Finding a new set of friends may also come with changing jobs or rethinking where you live—which is exactly what happened for me in the aftermath of my Deep Shift, and it's something I see a lot. All I had to do was keep following my intuition—that quiet voice inside gently guiding me in the next right steps to take. I also found it easier to tune into this voice after my

Post-Shift Friendship Guidelines

Rule #1 Be *open* to finding your new tribe. Go to classes, join groups, check out bulletin boards (both online and at your local coffee shop, deli, or independent bookstore), and branch out to find people who align with your new way of being.

Rule #2 When you do meet new peeps who you feel drawn to, carve out some time to get to know them. Meet up for coffee or go for a meal. Take a walk together in a nearby park. Go on a hike! A quick "hello" at a workshop is one thing, but real connection takes time and effort to foster, so go big or go home.

Rule #3 Never forget that friendships are precious. Social media has made "friends" seem sort of throwaway, but the importance of having deep platonic relationships with like-minded individuals cannot be underestimated. Nurture them consistently with love, respect, and a large dose of fun! These connections will enrich you in ways that go beyond words.

trip to Opposite Land had wiped out all the conditioning that told me life "should" look a certain way.

I basically realized that if I just trusted and followed my intuition, things would fall into place without me even trying—something that became clear after I discovered that working overtime to have everything "figured out" before making any moves was a loser's game that led to a ho-hum type of existence. For me, the juice would really flow when I was able to put down my thinking cap and totally commit to following my bliss wherever it led me—even if on paper, what my intuition was telling me made zero sense.

After trying this a few times and winding up with a *way* better outcome than I could ever have come up with on my own, I began to trust that my intuition knew exactly what to do, all the time. If I just followed my inner compass, all sorts of doors would open. Easy-peasy. Sorta.

Lord knows, it can be hard to trust your gut. But today is a new day, and going forward I encourage you to make your intuition your ride-or-die. You can and must learn to lean on it, believe in it, and act on it. This is perhaps THE most important lesson of Deep Shift. In literally showing you that you are never truly in control, and that no matter how many "facts" you can gather before you act the Universe is still gonna throw you for a gigantic curveball, it has been showing you all along that all you can rely on is your instincts about what's right for you. Let me show you what I mean.

Follow Your Dreams

In my case, it all started with a dream. Literally. One night as I again slept like a baby (did I mention how Deep Shift healed my crippling fourteen-year sleep disorder?), I dreamed I lived in a cedar house, off a gravel road with a green street sign that had "155th" written on it.

Side note: getting important information in our dreams is another Shifter superpower. This means that any time I have a dream I can clearly remember when I wake up, I pay attention. In fact, you may notice that you feel more connected to your dreams both during and after Deep Shift, as your subconscious reaches out to guide you, fuel you with information, and expand your awareness. *Your* job is to pay attention. Consider writing down your dreams and reflecting on the feelings that were present in them. Often, it's not the specific details but the emotions the dream brings up that have the big message for you.

But I digress. Back to the cedar house on 155th Street. I had that dream in March of 2013, and in the coming days and weeks I would find myself reliving it in my mind's eye. I had no idea what it meant, and I also wasn't trying to figure it out (remember, I'd decided that *thinking is overrated*). But for some reason, the dream about the cedar home on the gravel road stuck with me.

Fast-forward to the July fourth weekend that same year, when the idea popped into my head to take a trip. That morning. Talk about short notice. I still had no idea where I was going to spend the weekend, but I proceeded to pack up my car, fill my tank with gas, and get Frida, my little Chihuahua, all situated for a road trip. I literally started driving with no plan. By that point in my Shift, I felt extremely free. I wasn't scared to travel alone; in fact, I preferred it. I also felt a strong pull to new experiences because it seemed to fuel that magical energy inside of me. And I'd learned to completely trust my intuition because it never let me down. When I followed my gut, life just got cooler and cooler. Hitting the road that day "just because" was a no-brainer.

As I cruised down the highway heading out of Chicago, I thought to myself, "Okay, I'm going to call the only bed-and-breakfast I know in Fairfield, Iowa. If they allow dogs and they have a vacancy, I'll go there. If that doesn't work out, I'll head to Lexington, Kentucky, and hang out there for the weekend." It was as simple as that. I love horse country in Kentucky, and I was also smitten with Fairfield, a magical little town in southeast Iowa. Neither place was far from Chicago, and either would make for a chill weekend getaway. A win-win situation either way.

Well, the Universe certainly had some cool plans for me. After pointing my car south and driving like a Muppet toward wherever, my cell phone rang. It was the woman from the great bed-and-breakfast in Fairfield. She informed me she normally didn't allow pets (boo!) but that I would be her last guest, since she was selling the B&B a week later. She said she could make an exception for Frida because she was already on her way out of the business.

I had my answer; I pointed the car toward Iowa and drove.

I knew about three people in this cool-ass community about five hours west of Chicago, and I gave one of my new friends a buzz and told him I would be in town later that afternoon. He promptly invited me for pizza and fireworks by the town square. I was all in.

By that evening, I was sitting outside a great café, having a glass of pinot noir and a couple of slices (I was still playing with my new Shifter diet at this point). I was chatting it up with some people I'd been introduced to when out of nowhere, up walks one of my closest friends from Chicago, Mary. I almost fell over when I saw her!

I blurted out, "What are you doing here?"

Turns out she'd recently bought a house in town and had had the same urge as me to get out of Chicago for the weekend. So, she'd jumped in her car on a moment's notice and headed to Iowa, just as I had done.

I couldn't believe Mary had bought a house in this farm-country whistle-stop! I'd never considered making a move like that . . . or had I? I had a blast that night, hanging out with Mary and meeting a bunch of chill, way-hip spiritual people, and when I got back to my bed-and-breakfast I started looking up homes to rent. I liked the vibe here, a lot, and while I didn't have any plans to leave Chicago and move to middle-of-nowhere Iowa, I was just following my curiosity (again!).

Then I saw a house out in the country for rent, on thirteen acres, and the place looked really nice. I thought, *What the hell! I'm in town, I might as well go look at it.* After emailing the owner, I put away my laptop and drifted off to sleep. The next morning, I woke up to an email with a slot to see the country house at 3 p.m. that day. Perfect. This gave me time to meet Mary for coffee, grab lunch with another new friend, and explore the town a bit more.

When I showed up for coffee with Mary, I told her about the house I was going to go see that afternoon. I explained that when she told me she'd bought a house in the country, it got me thinking it could be fun to look at some houses in the area. When I let her know the address, she replied, "That's my neighbor's house!" WHAT in God's name was going on?!

Mary described the house as being super-cute and said the land out there was amazing. We laughed about how fun it would be to be neighbors and have adventures in some wide-open spaces. It sounded like a blast. But, I mean, let's get real. I wasn't going to give up my gorgeous condo and my life in the city and move out to the Iowan wilderness . . . *or was I?*

Anyway, driving to my 3 p.m. showing, my GPS brought me to a long gravel road, which was apparently leading me in the direction of the house. Then, as I turned onto the street the house was on, I looked up and realized that the crossroad sign read "155th Street." Okay, the Universe was full-on FREAKING me out now. And when I pulled into the long gravel driveway leading to the house, my mind was further blown. Cuz what do you think I was staring at there in front of me? Yup, a big brown cedar house!

On the inside, I honestly felt like I was one with the whole Cosmos and that this symphony that was my life was just a magic machine. I was shocked, excited, filled with life, and totally all in. I now knew for CERTAIN that the Universe was running the show, and it was fucking exhilarating. Fifteen minutes later, I signed a twelve-month lease. Without thinking it through (yep, overrated), without knowing how I was going to pay for it, with no idea about what the hell I was going to do in Iowa, without anything. I simply followed the signs, trusted myself and the Cosmos, and went for it.

People, it was one of the best moves I've ever made.

Not least because it was also directly connected to the career shift that had come on the heels of my Deep Shift. In the few months prior to the cedar house serendipity, I'd had the idea to write a book. I had no clue how I would do that while working full time, but I knew it was on the horizon for me. Since I'd now signed a lease that began in a couple of weeks, I had to make some serious decisions. This meant it was time to go inward again, use all the tools I had picked up from my Deep Shift, and plunge into Shifter 2.0 mode.

What did I REALLY want for my life going forward? That was the question I asked myself. How did I want to live, what did I want to do with my days, and who did I want to be? After sleeping on it for a night, I woke up knowing exactly what to do. I was going to put in my two weeks' notice, sell everything I owned, move to Iowa (full time!), and write my first book. In that order.

The next day I let my boss know about my plans. I told her how much I had loved my job, and that I appreciated all the opportunities she had given me, but that it was time to go out on my own. I gave her a couple of weeks' notice and planned on working overtime to help her with anything she needed and to help her find my replacement. My next step was to sell all my stuff and get my condo rented. Within days of posting my furniture on Facebook and Craigslist, it was all sold. Within one day of listing my condo for rent, a wonderful couple signed a lease. And so in less than two weeks, I found myself on the road to my new life. Just like that, my new journey had begun.

So why am I telling you all of this? First of all, there's nothing special about me that meant things worked out so swiftly and easily when I decided to follow my dreams. Yes, I had some savings, and selling all my stuff covered the cost of my move. I also don't have kids, which meant I was free to essentially blow up my life and change my whole situation on a dime. I appreciate that this was all a HUGE plus, and that not everybody reading this book will have this freedom. But following your dreams could also be as simple as turning your back on a toxic relationship, doing some online research into a subject that has always fascinated you, or committing to reading one mind-expanding book a month. I also didn't use any fancy juju to consciously manifest the big life changes that I experienced; all I did was follow my instincts, no questions asked; instincts that each and every human on the planet is equipped with.

Unsure where to start? You can begin by writing out a dream that seems so far-fetched it's never going to happen, and then imagine the far-out circumstances that would need to align for it to come true. Go really out there, as if no coincidence is too magical or "meant to be." Next, write out the steps you would need to take to make your dream a reality, even if it seems totally unattainable at this point in your life. The point is to get yourself to picture a world in which everything aligns and all your dreams come true. The act of seeing it all unfolding in your mind is a powerful step to believing it can all happen for you.

The fact is, the Universe works with its own set of rules, and when we tune our inner radar to this cosmic signal, anything (and everything) is possible. Pre–Deep Shift, we're often so caught up in all the humdrum man-made rules that we're not conscious of the magic that's unfolding around us at all times.

When you've been to Opposite Land and back, all bets as to what a "normal" life should look like are off, which makes it easier to let the Cosmos, the energy of the Universe, and the laws of Almighty Nature do their thing. There's no more forcing things—and if you can just keep showing up for Shifter duty *without overthinking it*, you will find that you are aligned with the all-powerful force that guides all life, the energy that runs through the veins of every living thing on the planet. Simply sit back, follow the signs, and allow them to lead you directly to the new people, projects, and places that are meant for you.

How is this possible? Because Deep Shift has shown you, in no uncertain terms, that you are NOT the one in control here. My mom had raised me to "let go and let God." When I experienced Deep Shift, this idea was no longer a theory; it became my reality. This made life so much easier. Meditation was the daily practice that helped me tune in, and the rest was just about living. Having fun, being free, and trusting that all would be well. Which sounds a little scary but is actually a lot easier and more relaxing than overthinking every single decision that you make. Trust me.

Because now? You're following a different set of rules—and yes, this way of living is so different from how we've been taught to get things done that it often feels like magic. This is the true gift of going through Deep Shift. You come out the other side a new person. A person who marches to the beat of their own drum. Who knows their dreams aren't random. Who lives by their instincts, takes action on their intuition, and who, literally, experiences *unimaginable* good fortune on a regular basis. No effort required, no strings attached.

A New Path Forward

Okay, so hopefully all this is encouraging you to embrace whatever new path you may find yourself on post-Shift, and to really go for it full force. Honestly though, this is your only option, because now that the floodgates of transformation have opened, *there is no going back.* This is the way of the Shifter. *We were born to transform.* This means acting on your intuition, following your dreams, and not giving a rat's ass about how everyone else is doing things. You're following your own program now, baby. You have crossed the Rubicon, and your Deep Shift has prepared you for an *extra-ordinary* life. And as scary as this can feel, I'm here to tell you that you got this.

As for how my whole "Iowa adventure" turned out? Well, one thing's for sure: it totally changed my life. New friends, a new career, and a new home—it ticked every single box. As I've said before (and I'll very likely say again), Iowa is where I met my soul family. I was welcomed to my new life by a group of individuals who are so extraordinary, so unique, and so full of love that I consider myself the luckiest gal on the planet to count them as my people.

On the career front, I went ahead and wrote that book, *Enlightenment Is Sexy*, which (along with my blogging) turned out to be the start of a writing career. Soon after I settled into my new place, I would take myself to the same coffee shop each day, sit at the same table, put my headphones on, and write. I had never written a book before, but the words just flowed out of me. It was through my new connections that I met an amazing editor, Willy Mathes, and with him by my side, I wrote a book I'm extremely proud of. I became an *author!* Me! Who had always loved books but would have never dreamed in a million years that I would end up writing one. As if a cosmic domino effect was at play, following my gut about that one dream about the cedar house had paid off in spades.

Perhaps you're thinking, "Good for you, Val, you got really lucky. Nothing like this is going to happen to me." But think about it; it likely already has. A random encounter with somebody led to you getting a new job; a dream has felt like it had a clear message for you (regardless of whether you followed through); or even just having "a feeling" about a certain individual, or "knowing" something is going to turn out a certain way. We're always evolving (especially us Shifters), and everything that's ever happened to you was because the Universe designed it that way. The difference is that now there's no resisting the flow, which just makes it easier and more enjoyable to ride the waves of change.

Whatever happens in life, there is also *never* any going back. After Deep Shift, this is amplified—as the bigger and more sudden or intense the changes, the more aware we are of all that we're leaving behind. But me moving to Iowa was really no different from me going to college or starting my first job. It just felt more magical because it wasn't part of the "socially approved" life plan.

With your new post-Shift kaleidoscope eyes, you're more likely to spot and follow the signs that might have passed you by while you were sleepwalking through life. When you're following a script, there's not much space for improvisation—and that's all this really is. Instead of reciting the lines you've been given, Deep Shift has wiped the slate clean and given you permission to make things up as you go along. The new rules are . . . there are no rules! Oh, and just say YES! to whatever feels like a glowing green light in your soul.

If my Iowa adventure showed me anything, it's that when you let go of how things "should" play out is when all these other possibilities open up. Now THAT is what I call freedom.

Thinking back to your old life, it's also natural to feel some sadness about what you've left behind. They were some good times! But when you reeeee- aaaaalllly think about it (or rather *feel* into it), were you really, truly happy? On every level? If you stopped most people in the street and asked them if they were completely satisfied with their life, chances are they'd say no. Because most of us, on some level, spend our whole lives making do with the circumstances we've been given versus dreaming and taking a risk on living out our wildest dreams. In my case, literally!

How about, in showing you that everything you thought you knew was wrong, Deep Shift has taken everything away . . . so that the Universe could give you something even better? Something you can't even imagine for your-self yet?

On the heels of my Deep Shift, I felt like I was starting life all over again in the most exciting, exhilarating, and enlivening way possible. It was like getting two lives for the price of one! And it all happened because I took a chance and said YES! even (scratch that: *especially*) when I didn't have all the answers. Along the way, I meditated, I prayed a lot, I journaled, and I asked for guidance. I did everything I could to stay grounded and in my body. I had my spiritual healing team on speed-dial. I surrounded myself with people who validated me and made me feel safe and loved. And above all, I allowed myself to trust that it would all work out. After all, I'd survived the worst of the worst—losing my beautiful mom—and I'd come out stronger and more "me" than ever.

And this is the way of the Shifter. A life filled with equal parts trials and challenges and magic and surprises. Often this means not knowing *exactly* where you're going next, but knowing that it's *always* going to be one hell of a ride. As I like to say, "It's time to take life by the balls and go for it." If sur-viving *your* Deep Shift has shown you anything, I hope it's that everything you need is within you. That you have the tools. That you have the power and you have the knowledge. That, as a Shifter, you are a child of God. A warrior for peace and love. That you are the embodiment of life itself.

CHAPTER 9

Welcome to the Other Side

"Throw your dreams into space like a kite, and you
do not know what it will bring back, a new life, a
new friend, a new love, a new country."

Anaïs Nin

the thing about being in Deep Shift is that *it cannot last forever*. It might feel like it while you're in it (cut to you wringing your hands, asking, *When is this all gonna end?*), but the day will surely come when it's time to learn how to "human" again. Not that you're exactly the same human as when we started. As the waves of change begin to settle and the clouds part above, it's time to fully engage with the world as the completely new (and improved) version of yourself.

The good news is that if you've been following along closely, you should now be armed with all the tools you need to go out and grab your new reality by the balls. Even better, everything you've experienced thus far has shown you that you were *made* for a life filled with wonder, excitement, and a massive dose of magic. To all my fellow Shifters, your time has come!

Think about it for a minute. Anybody who's been through Deep Shift—and believe me, there are more of us out there than you think—has basically been to hell and back again. This will likely result in a person taking a deep dive into revamping their spiritual life, their relationships, their career, even where they live. Everything, and I mean *everything*, has been up for grabs. Once life has shown you that everything you thought you knew was wrong, you have nothing to lose when it comes to creating a new life that fits the new you like a sparkly, rhinestone-studded glove.

If anything, being in Deep Shift shows us that unhappiness and stress come from trying to completely control all aspects of your life. As Shifters, we've pretty much always known that the only way to roll is with the punches. Then along comes Deep Shift to show us that resistance to the waves of change is not only futile, it can keep us stuck in pain, confusion, and doubt. By taking everything we thought we knew about who we are, what's important to us, where our security comes from, and how to navigate the world we live in, and putting it in the great big blender in the sky, the Universe has basically been teaching us that *all we can control are our responses to what life throws at us*. And coming out the other side is when you get to put it into action.

The coolest thing of all? Having cleaned all the crap out of your life and kicked tired old habits and behaviors to the curb, now is also the time to take your heightened powers of manifestation, intuition, and *magic* for a test-drive. Being in Deep Shift has essentially been a process of fine-tuning and upgrading your operating system, and now that the dust is beginning to settle, it's time to see what your revamped mind/body time-and-space machine can do!

For starters, you may find that music sounds better, food tastes better, and connections feel deeper. You may also find you have developed "supernatural" abilities, such as feeling more psychic, manifesting things in real time, an uncanny ability to see people for who they really are, having experiences with people who have passed away, and lucid dreaming. The list goes on and on. So let's take a look at what the "new you" can do!

It Ain't Over 'til It's Over

But first of all, how do you know when you're coming out of Deep Shift and landing on the other side? All I can say is, you will feel it in your bones. Everything will just start coming together, and your confidence will be off the charts. Best of all, you will start to feel like you know, without a shadow of a doubt, who you are and why you're here on the planet. And no matter what wild times you've been through, you'll also begin to experience an incredible sense of appreciation for your Shift. The biggest gift of having made it through? A crystal-clear sensation of being whole and complete.

Which is not to say you won't experience another Deep Shift in your life. Once a Shifter, always a Shifter! But before we get ahead of ourselves, here are some signs to look out for that you're coming out the other side:

- Feeling more centered and sure of yourself. You've experienced the guidance of the Universe firsthand, and you KNOW it has your back.

- Life no longer feels out of control. Little things no longer turn into big things.

- You're making much more confident decisions and no longer second-guessing yourself since your intuition game is *on*.

- Your sleeping is on track, and you're not so sensitive to different foods. Things feel calmer and quieter in your mind and body.

- You're more light-hearted and sociable, and less reactive. Your entire nervous system is also calmer.

- Things that made you feel nervous now generate excitement in you.

I can remember the exhilarating feeling of finally hitting my stride after years of being in Deep Shift. It was as though everything started to make sense again, and a bolder me had emerged from a cocoon. But when I was deep in the Shift, I remember often wondering if I would ever be "normal" again. Looking back, I can't help but think, "Wow, you were that bad-ass who just kept going, even when there was seemingly no end in sight."

Well, dear Shifters, I'm here to tell you there *is* an end in sight . . . and that this end is your new beginning. When my beautiful mother reminded me, "Val, the bad never stays bad forever," what she forgot to add is that if you're a warrior who has found the strength to keep going even when the going got tough, you will be rewarded. The prize is freedom like you have never experienced it before, because it comes from the inside. It is the freedom to live as the person you were always meant to be. You have come into your own, and it's incredible.

Ultimately, this is the result of detaching from the outcomes and leaving the results to the Universe itself. In my case, this became a sort of game for me. Faced with every and any opportunity that presented itself, I would wonder to myself, "What if I just go for it? What will happen?" It was literally like playing a video game. My strategy? Tune in to what my body (a.k.a. God) is telling me and go boldly forth as if all the potential outcomes were good. As if every YES! would lead me to exactly where I needed to be, even if this looked nothing like I would have planned for myself. Confident in my ability to handle whatever came my way, I was no longer bogged down by "what ifs." I wasn't in it for anything special except for the ride. And on the flipside, living in tune with my intuition meant I also found it far easier to say NO to anything that wasn't a HELL YES! Talk about a way to save a bunch of time and energy!

On the other side of Deep Shift, you will likely find your confidence and your spirits riding high. You've proven to the Universe just how resilient and chill you are in the face of whatever Shift it throws your way. When you feel strong and ready to engage with the world, life is going to meet you where you're at. So, people, get ready for some seriously good times!

To the Manifestation Station

First and foremost, the path has now been cleared for you to get clear on what you *really* want for your life. Given that you have also been undoing all the societal brainwashing that comes with living on this planet, what comes up when you really feel into this might surprise you at first. But like Danny Kaye once so wisely said, "Life is a great big canvas, and you should throw all the paint on it you can." This means it's time to get your hands dirty and color the hell out of your world. And no, you don't have to stay inside the lines. This is your time. You are the writer, the producer, the director, and the star of your very own Shifter reality show. It's time to put your new wizard-level abilities to use and set about imagining your dream life.

My Deep Shift found me engaging with DEEP inner work, making major life changes, and being brutally honest with myself and the people around me. It was when I finally began integrating all the superpowers I'd picked up along the way that my life took off like a rocket. Lo and behold, going through the Shift had turned me into a *master manifester*. I would literally think of something I wanted, and very quickly it would become my reality. It was almost freaky and a bit shocking at first, but then it just became *who I was*. This is how things roll with me to this day. For Shifters, the art of manifestation begins and ends with our intuition. You have learned to trust your intuition, yes? So what's that inner voice saying? What's coming up for you? Do you have a strong urge to start your own business? Do you want to get your shit together in order to meet the partner of your wildest dreams? Are you ready to buy yourself a home you adore? At this point, anything is possible! You just have to put your attention to clarifying your wants and needs, then let your Higher Power/God/the Universe do its magic. If any actions on your part are required to help things along, trust that you'll get "a sign" and that you'll know exactly what it's telling you to do (or *not* do).

Deep Shift has shown you beyond a shadow of a doubt that your second sight is directly connected to your inner compass. You now know that every instinct or "hit" is leading you in the direction of your best life, meaning the one where you get to live 100 percent as your TRUE self. Your job is to stay grounded, stay in the flow, and follow your intuition's lead in terms of the next actions to take. And I tell you, you'll be shocked how much you can accomplish with all the new Universal support you're getting.

Now, I've always been a dreamer and a person with big ideas. But it wasn't until I went through my radical personal transformation, my own Deep Shift, that I really had a fire under my ass. Going to hell and back, including, in my case, surviving a total Spiritual Emergency, had left me basically fearless. In addition to seeing the world from a completely different, much more expansive perspective, this gave me the green light to simply be true to myself and go for it. After all, what did I have to lose? What I discovered is that as long as you're grounded, of sound mind and body, and in tune with your true inner voice, you can manifest anything. And I mean *anything*.

But first, let me be clear: this is not your grandma's "manifestation" I'm talking about. Books like *The Secret* put the emphasis on coming up with something specific to manifest, and then attempting to "align your energy" with whatever that thing is. What I'm talking about is *literally* the opposite (because we're in Opposite Land, remember?). Instead of asking the Universe for a red Corvette, this is about forgetting what you think you want and handing it over to the Divine power to surprise you with something even better.

Rather than trying to manipulate the all-knowing forces of the Universe into giving you what you think you want, you will be given all that is yours to have, and that's it. It may not sound as cool, but trust me, setting yourself free from cravings and focusing instead on what's right in front of you, from moment to magical moment, will bring more gifts into your life than a thousand Santas.

There is also a formula I follow. It's easy-breezy to follow and it works like a charm:

Step 1: Listen very closely to what is coming up within you. What's grabbing your attention? Are you feeling an urge to write a book? Visit a new country? Save a certain amount of money? It doesn't matter what the desire is. What matters is that you tune in to hear the call.

Step 2: Respect the information you're getting. Understand that *nothing* is too wild or outlandish. You are now operating with an entirely new system, one in which the Universe is totally onboard with you and whatever impulses are firing in your heart and soul. You're thinking and operating outside of the box now. You aren't doing things like everyone else. The deprogramming has found you carving out your own path. This means new opportunities and experiences are on their way.

Step 3: Take action. Once you know what you want, if your inner voice says "Jump!" . . . you jump! When you're tuned into the Cosmos, you'll likely find yourself doing things you would never have done before *just because*. Maybe this means striking up a conversation with a random stranger who, it turns out, can help get your art into a local gallery. Maybe it will find you making YouTube videos to sell your amazing new product. Or ditching your dating apps and asking somebody you met on the train on a date. Totally go all in. Not only will you feel exhilarated, but you'll have a blast working toward your goals, because you'll be moving toward your dreams with the winds of the Universe at your back.

Step 4: Keep the pedal to the metal. Soon enough, you will find people just showing up to help you, amazing connections falling into your lap, and doors opening where previously you thought there were only walls. When this starts happening, *lean in*. When this magic begins showing up in your life, it can be natural not to trust it at first. But remember, each "sign" is another green light! God's way of showing you that you're on the right path. Now is the time to gun it through each intersection. Soon you'll be feeling the euphoria of being in alignment with the Cosmos and your true nature.

Step 5: Don't let anyone stop you from trusting your gut and going for it. If you're around people who you instinctively know can't handle your new mojo, just don't tell them. Chances are, they'll only try to bring you down— even if they see it as trying to keep you safe. But they can't see your vision, and so they'll never understand when you try to explain where you're going. Having been through Deep Shift, you'll eventually be surrounded by a tribe of peeps who truly get you. And besides, you've already proven to yourself that you can handle anything. Boom.

Magic, Miracles, and All That Jazz

Okay, you may be noticing that not only is your approach to life significantly *different*, but your "Spidey senses" are different, too. As in, you're more in tune with everything around you. Music sounds crisper and more all-enveloping, your vision is clearer, and every single connection feels deeper. You are in tune with nature, and the world around you is playing ball, supporting you each step of the way.

So what does it look and feel like when you're actually living in a reality where "the (*Star Wars*) Force is with you"? Well, as I noted earlier, it's seeing the world with new eyes and hearing with new ears. But it can also be more than that. *Way* more. Abilities may come to the surface that you may have never known were possible. Referred to as *siddhis* in ancient Indian texts known as the Vedas, these are actual supernormal perceptual states. These "magical powers" (which I've listed further on in this chapter) can spontaneously begin developing in a person who has gone through the Deep

Shift wormhole and come out the other side. Once underway, in time they become your new norm.

If and when this starts happening to you, it can seem odd or even shocking. But after you let yourself settle into this awakened, breakthrough state of being, having "superpowers" just becomes part of who you are. Like everything else, you begin to integrate these new abilities, till they become your soup of the day. How you travel through the world. In fact, it's not something you will even be interested in talking about. It will just be.

When I talk about these supernormal states, what am I actually referring to? To start with, psychic abilities (e.g., telepathy, clairvoyance); out-of-the-box experiences where you're intuitively guided into events with such perfectly timed serendipities you're left freakin' speechless; extraordinary capabilities, such as knowing *way* more than what the five senses or even a highly intelligent mind can behold; and using your body's innate strengths and capabilities to achieve miraculous, even "superhuman" results. All of which may well become part and parcel of the post–Deep Shifter's daily experience of life.

For example, you may find yourself wondering, "How am I going to get outta sitting here at the dinner table on Thanksgiving with my drunk Uncle Joe?" Well, being in tune with Universal consciousness and the laws of nature, your "wish" is its command. Next thing you know, your phone rings, and it's an unexpected call from a friend saying they really need your help, cuz their car broke down and could you come pick them up? Voila! No more drunk Uncle Joe ranting in your ear!

Now, some of these abilities may evolve naturally by virtue of your having made it through your Deep Shift to a more awakened consciousness. But they can also be cultivated in more deliberate ways, through the use of yoga and/or meditation, for example.

In my case, as soon as I started meditating regularly, I began to notice I was able to connect with people who had passed away. The first time it happened, it came in the form of a dream. But not just *any* dream; even though I was sleeping, I felt like I was fully "awake." In the dream, my mother came to me and explained my purpose on this Earth, including why I could see her when other people couldn't, and what my future would look like.

She then continued coming to me in an ongoing series of dreams, describing to me what the afterlife looked like and what I could expect, which helped completely wipe away my fear of death.

Soon after this, I began to regularly "watch" myself sleep, hovering over my body and just observing my physical self. I wasn't scared, I was just curious. This kind of witnessing is what Deepak Chopra calls "the presence of awareness during sleep"—and little did I know it at the time, but it is one of the stages of developing higher states of consciousness.

Sure enough, as I integrated the experiences of my Deep Shift, these extraordinary abilities started to show up with increased regularity. In my case, having always been super-sensitive and intuitive, and having had a mom who'd taught me to be so open-minded about all things spiritual, it felt as though skills that had been lying dormant in my life were now bubbling up to the surface.

But luckily, I also had a friend who I could discuss these topics with without them freaking out! He'd been through his own personal Deep Shift and had also experienced these states of awakening. Luckily for him, he had a spiritual teacher who'd helped him navigate forward, so he knew exactly what was happening with me. Being able to discuss my newfound abilities with someone who truly "got it" helped me so, so much.

If you're having experiences like the ones I'm referring to (or whenever you do) and you don't have a friend or personal contact who is sufficiently experienced and knowledgeable about such matters, it would be a good move on your part to seek out a transpersonal psychologist. This particular type of therapist is trained in nonordinary states of consciousness and will know exactly what you're talking about when you tell them you flew across your bedroom while meditating (for example!). If this is not accessible to you, then reading up on the phenomenon, especially the accounts of others who have experienced these states, will help you better understand what's going on.

In order to get a real eyeful of what's possible, let's look at some of the other siddhis, or extraordinary powers, described in the yoga sutras. According to ancient scripture that's backed up by historical accounts, some of the amazing feats accomplished by enlightened Master Shifters (my terminology) include:

The Five Inferior Siddhis

1. You can know the future, present, and past.

2. You are unaffected by dualities, like cold and heat.

3. You can know the thoughts of others.

4. You can stop the effects of water, fire, and poison.

5. You cannot be conquered by others.

The Ten Secondary Siddhis

1. You are not bothered by thirst, hunger, or other physical appetites.

2. You can hear distant sounds and conversations.

3. You can see distant events.

4. You can travel to any location instantly, just by thinking of the spot.

5. You can become any shape or being you want.

6. You can enter anyone's body anytime you want.

7. You can choose when you will die.

8. You can watch the activities of beings in other realms or dimensions.

9. Any event you desire to happen will happen.

10. Your spoken words become reality.

The Eight Primary Siddhis

1. **Anima Siddhi:** You become able to be smaller than the smallest subatomic energy particle. You can go inside or through objects.

2. **Mahima Siddhi:** You can be as large as the universe.

3. **Laghima Siddhi:** You can become any frequency of light and travel in light.

4. **Prapti Siddhi:** You can call any object forth from emptiness.

5. **Prakamya Siddhi:** You can fulfill any desire you have.

6. **Ishita Siddhi:** You can appear to defy the laws of nature by walking on fire or water, breathing fire, and so on.

7. **Vashita Siddhi:** You can control other beings' actions.

8. **Kamavasayita Siddhi:** You can do anything. This highest of siddhis contains most of the others.

I love this breakdown of all the different levels of supernatural abilities. If you're post–Deep Shift, you may have already begun experiencing a couple of the five inferior siddhis—which are relatively common, with many people experiencing one or more of them. During and after my Deep Shift, I could (clear as day) know the thoughts of others, hear distant sounds and conversations, and often felt like I could not be "conquered" by others. Now those strengths are old shoe to me. They have just become who I am. Meanwhile, the secondary siddhis are said to come to many in the natural course of their spiritual growth, and only highly skilled, advanced practitioners attain the eight primary siddhis. Those who do have access to the higher siddhis very seldom reveal their accomplishment.

Some fascinating stuff, can we agree? And for those of us Shifters who have experienced some of them, perhaps you are beginning to believe that anything and everything truly is possible. That there is no ceiling when it comes to what we as Shifters are capable of. Going through Deep Shift means we have opened the door to a world full of potential. We are awake, we have expanded awareness, and we are in tune with the laws of nature. It's all happening. Bring. It. On.

Keeping the Juju Flowing

Ultimately, responding to your inner prompts without being attached to outcomes and staying open to the totally magical, miraculous happenings all around you is how you attract the highest and best possibilities for your life. And while this way of being can feel clunky at first, with enough practice it will become effortless. We've been taught that we have to work for what we want; that "success" is directly linked to the level of effort that we put in. Now, though, you're discovering that you are doing your part by simply moving your feet forward according to your heart's desires. This *only* works if you aren't a prisoner to the end result. Yes, you are the star of the movie of your life, but with a twist. Nobody gave you a script.

Remember, relinquishing control of everything *except* our responses to life is the only way to live as active participants and co-creators of our reality, a.k.a. this short-lived thing that we call life.

I like to joke with people that they might as well go out and do all the things they truly want to do, because, y'know, they'll be dead before they know it! This tends to get me some pretty shocked looks from whoever I'm talking to. But take it from me: as somebody who has lost way too many friends and family members, I am very aware of how short life is. Which has only doubled my commitment to making the absolute most of the time I've got.

Life is really just a blink of an eye. So why settle for anything less than exactly what you want? Why not walk away from anything that's holding you down or making you feel like shit, and fill your life up with things that bring you joy, love, and adventure instead? The coolest part is that anybody who has been through Deep Shift, as painful and confusing as it might have felt at times, has been gifted with a profound, visceral understanding of this truth. Which is the truth about who we really are, what we're really here to experience, and how the world really works. Again, I like to think this sets us apart from the riffraff. We did the work, and now we get to reap the rewards. Joy! Joy! Joy!

I *know* you're probably *still* thinking, "Yeah, easier said than done."

You're right. It will be hard at times, but trust me. Once you begin to emerge from the turbulence of your personal Deep Shift and start to practice living this way, it will become second nature to you and you won't even have to think about it. You'll begin to move through your life in a state of flow, instead of pushing and clawing your way through your days. That's just how we Deep Shifters roll. We are all power (Cosmic power) and no force.

Ram Dass, one of my favorite Shifters of all time, said it best: "If you understand enough about where you are going, everything becomes a vehicle through which you get free." Quite simply put (as if you didn't know this already), the old rules no longer apply to you. And the sooner you can embody this memo, the sooner you'll be able "to human" (as a verb) on a higher level. Yes, life is going to try to pull you back into your old ways, but you have become untouchable and you know it. The odd part is that the world now knows it too.

When I was moving through this stage of my Deep Shift, I was told by a close friend that there were dark forces in the world that would try to pull me away from living my truth. I remember being really shocked, and thinking, "Seriously, there's evil out there that's trying to hurt me?" But I've come to realize what my friend was actually trying to tell me. The "dark" forces are society at large and the mental conditioning that human beings have been subjected to over centuries of domination and control.

Think about it. If you spend all night watching the news, you will very quickly go to a dark place. Everything reported by the major news networks is all bad, all the time. They literally have reporters positioned all around the world, reporting back on horrible events happening in faraway places and beaming them right into our living rooms. Yes, it's important to be informed. But ultimately this just programs us to be on the lookout for disaster around every corner. Not least because this creates an addictive chemical reaction in our bodies that basically keeps us hooked. But, like, what's happening right outside your window? Take a look right now. Is the world really such a terrible place?

The other "dark forces" to watch out for? The external and internal distractions that keep us from walking our true path. These may come in the form of friends who want you to follow along with what they're doing instead of breaking off and staking your own path. But these can also show up as residual inner feelings of self-doubt. When it comes to developing the concentration and awareness to rise above all of this and stay in your magical Shifter lane, Gandhi said it best: "I won't allow anyone to walk through my mind with their dirty feet." Once you have been through Deep Shift, you need to keep your mind and your consciousness as clean as a whistle.

One thing is for certain: your life will never look the same again. But why would you want it to?! It's a new day for you, and the doors to a life filled with wonder and expanded awareness have been blown open. You are in for the ride of your life. Enjoy every moment of it!

CHAPTER 10

Your Real-World Maintenance Plan

"In the kind of world we have today, transformation of
humanity might well be our only real hope for survival."

Stanislav Grof

by the time you have gotten your Shift together to the best of your
ability, you will once again feel like your feet are firmly planted on
the ground. You know who you are and have a good sense of where
you're headed. You will be able to put your faith and trust in the grand plans
the Universe has in store for you. And you are on your way to a new life, a
new way of being, and a truckload of new experiences. So how to stay true
to your Shifter path? What you need is a Real-World Maintenance Plan to
keep you on track.

For starters, the keys to your new life are *on the inside*. As Shifters, our
inner life is the best show in town. Living from this place is very different
from living from the outside in, and it's the opposite of how most people
do life. Rather than responding to external events, living "inside out" means
trusting your own inner compass first and foremost and letting your inner
knowing be your guide—and going through Deep Shift means you are now
primed for this.

Oh, and also? Living inside out is a giant old threat to the system that
allegedly makes this world spin. Those dark forces my friend spoke of in

the previous chapter (y'know, the angst-inducing stressors that prevent you from really LIVING by keeping you trapped in anxiety and self-doubt) can only influence you if your focus is mainly outward. Think about it: when you're not grounded in your inner knowing, every little thing will have the potential to influence your thinking and knock you off course. But tuning *in* first and foremost is not the same as tuning *out* what's happening in the world and sticking your head in the sand. Bad shit is always happening in the world; that will never stop. But when your gaze is turned toward your inner resources first and foremost, you will be able to remain solid and in control no matter what.

Going through a wild-ass Deep Shift experience has given you a lived example of this, to show you how it's done. And now that you're back in the "real world" (lol, yeah right, as if such a thing even exists!) it's on you to integrate everything you've learned, so that you can keep on bringing your full-tilt-boogie self to the world. In other words, now is when you get to come back down to earth and live life 200 percent! Bringing the inner to the outer, 24/7. Boom.

Because, the waves of change? They are also gonna keep a-comin'. Yes, you have now graduated to Alpha Shifter level, but when the going gets tough (and the going is going to keep getting tough), it can still take effort not to get sucked back into the normie way of doing things. This is where my Real-World Maintenance Plan comes in.

Remember how in chapter 4 I had you look at each area of your life and score where you were at on a scale of 1–10? Before we conclude our journey together, let's revisit each of these categories and look at how to make sure you are approaching them from the inside out, like the total pro that you are.

Career

Knowing what I know about the impact Deep Shift can have on a person's career trajectory, I would hazard a guess that you may already be in the midst of totally changing careers. That, or you have found a new appreciation for the wider potential impact of what you do for a living, and this has caused you to fall in love again with your current job. Either way, when it comes to how you utilize your talents and energetic output in the workforce, you're in a totally different space with a transformed, upgraded consciousness. Let's look at how to keep the mojo moving and maximize this moment.

Find your motivation. If I were a betting woman, my money would be on the fact that you are no longer just in it for the paycheck. Staying tuned in to what actually motivates you at work is essential for channeling your post-Shift energies into something that actually lights you up. Let your inner voice have a say in the matter. Follow its guidance and try not to be swayed by things like money and status—it could be that a lower-paying role is much better suited to what you actually want to do. Marry this with the natural drive to do the best work you can, whatever your field, and it will fulfill you and lead you to places you never knew possible.

Pay attention to how you feel before, during, and after your workday. Do you feel energized, exhausted, or just neutral? Do you wake up with a knot in your stomach, or looking forward to your day? Remember, our feelings don't lie. We are Shifters, and our energy is always showing us the way—our responsibility is to stay tuned in to it. As if it needs saying: "energized" is the ideal here, people! If you're feeling worn out or even just "meh" about your job, then it's time to either switch things up or find new ways to make it work for you.

Play the field. Do you spend time dreaming of doing something totally different than what you are currently doing? DO NOT IGNORE these thoughts. They are drops of information hitting your conscious mind and planting seeds of things to come. I'm not telling you to shit-can your job tomorrow and throw all caution to the wind. But I *am* advising you to pay attention and start to investigate whatever feels like "the next right thing" to do. Take the class, attend the workshop, chat it up with interesting person, or spend time focusing on a side hustle you've been cultivating, especially if it's something that could become a full-time gig. Respect and water these seeds, and they will blossom.

Home

You've likely had some seriously intense experiences as part of your personal transformation, and as a student of Deep Shift, you're going to continue to feel things deeply. All day, every day, you're going to be taking in a boatload of sensory information. For this reason, you need to come home to a palace of peace, even if that palace is a studio apartment in the middle of a bustling city. When you shut your front door, your whole body should have a sense of . . . well, having come *home*. How are you going to ensure that's what you've got?

Clean out your entire home. You heard me; every drawer, every cabinet, every corner of your home should be shed of all clutter. EVERYTHING MUST GO. For Shifters, the idea that "everything is energy" is very real: we can actually feel in our bones when the energy is off. Which means, all that crap in your house you never use? That's right, it's dirty, old energy that's crowding out the *clean, fresh* energy that will keep your home feeling mellow and serene. What to toss: any clothes you haven't worn in more than twelve months; books you never finished reading (or even got around to starting); kitchen gadgets you've used once and that are gathering dust in the back of a drawer. Anything from your old, pre-Shift existence, basically, which the shiny, post-Shift you no longer has space or use for in your life.

Invest in a new bed. Are you still sleeping on a mattress that holds all the secrets (and *whatever!*) of all your pre-Shift relationships and dark, misguided fantasies? Throw that shit out, too. You spend around one-third of your life in bed, so of course you want clear energy in your bedroom. That also goes for stained sheets, ripped towels, an old partner's sweater, and anything else that's lingering in your closet that energetically connects you to a past that is no longer part of your reality.

Now, fill your home with things you love. Do you continuously walk past a painting your aunt gave you . . . that you happen to dislike intensely? Replace it with a framed print by one of your favorite artists. Do fresh flowers make your heart sing? Don't wait for someone to give you some! Buy yourself a gorgeous bouquet and enjoy admiring them in your kitchen. Playing relaxing music (or any music you love) in your home will help keep the atmosphere attuned with the song in your soul. Regularly burn a nontoxic candle and stock up on your favorite fragrance of incense. Oh yeah, and spend LOTS of time meditating in your home. Filling the space with fresh, high-vibe energy will create an oasis of peace for yourself.

Just incorporating one of these things will help dramatically shift your energy. Start small and work toward the bigger things like a mattress.

Partnership

When we go through periods of change, especially changes this deep, nine times out of ten any serious relationships we're in will transform with us. But it could go one way or another. You may find you are falling even more deeply in love with your partner and reaching new levels of intimacy, or you may wake up knowing that it's time to leave your current relationship and move in a new direction.

Be honest with yourself. How are you feeling about your current partner and relationship? If you're single, how do you *really* feel about this? Regular-world conditioning tells us we "need" a partner to feel complete. Is this really the case for you? If you ask yourself straight-up, you will receive a clear answer. There's so much noise in our culture around relationships that getting really honest about what's right for us can be tricky. But your inner guidance is now clear as a bell. The challenge will be to actually act on what it's telling you.

Know what you want. Once you've established where you're at, either in a current relationship or thinking about your ideal partnership, you have to get crystal clear on what it is you actually want. The first step is to write it all out (a good, old-fashioned list will do) and then turn your attention to making it happen. And I mean list everything: Should he/she like cats, be good in bed, know how to cook? None of it is silly. When you identify all the things you want from a relationship, you may well find you have different needs, desires, and boundaries now that you've made it to the other side of your Deep Shift. Go deep, get real, and remember that your relationship with yourself is the most important thing here. What items on the list can you work on giving yourself first and foremost? How can you *become the list*?

Never lose your sense of self. No matter your current relationship status, having your own life separate from your partner's (or even from a best friendship) is going to be extremely important. You are a full-blown Shifter now, and your ideas, dreams, and desires are likely going to lead you down many new and different roads. Keeping some of that just for yourself will empower you, make you more attractive, and help you stay connected to your real sense of self. You are an individual first and foremost, and anybody you invite into your world needs to respect that.

Body

Your body is not just a lumpy meat suit; it truly IS your temple. For the time you are an inhabitant of this planet we call Earth, your body is also the home of your consciousness—which is what makes you, you. This means you'll want to keep it healthy and running like a fine-tuned engine, so your awareness (that is, your inner knowing) can just do its thing without being slowed down by a worn-out, broken-down, or glitchy body-machine. So let's recap on how to keep your body working smoothly, in tandem with your Shifter soul.

Break a sweat on the daily. When you have come out the other side of Deep Shift, loads of new energy will be coursing through your body—so the first thing you gotta get in the habit of doing is moving that vigor up and out so it doesn't trip you up. Energy is pow-er-full. You are now primed to direct it in ways that will help you create a more meaningful and lit-up life. But you don't want it building up in your system and blowing you out. Keep the flow going with regular (as in daily) walks, ideally in or as close to nature as you can get, and use it to propel you forward instead of spinning you out.

Treat food as your fuel. Don't eat a pile of crap. It's as simple as that, and you know *exactly* what I'm talking about. That old saying, "You are what you eat," is a Grade-A truth bomb. This means eat grounding foods, eat the rainbow (a healthy mix of fruits and veggies spanning lots of colors), and limit all processed, addictive, convenience foods (including supposedly healthy processed foods) that are essentially just *products* created to make somebody else rich. Along with daily movement, the food/fuel you choose is what will keep your body and mind in tip-top shape. Face it: if you're going to set the world on fire, fueling up at Taco Bell isn't going to get you very far.

Sleep. Get enough of it. Since Shifters are known for running energy at a high level during the day, you have to prioritize getting enough sleep. Why? So you can get up and do it all over again, duh! Plus, your dreams are likely to be much more magical now. Instead of feeling like you're missing out by turning in early, you can look forward to having your mind expanded in all kinds of ways by your dreams, with no effort required on your part whatsoever (and no hangover!). Once I was beyond the heavy-duty phase of my Deep Shift and started having really profound dreams, I couldn't wait to go to bed. You may even want to start a dream diary, jotting down a few keywords from your dreams up (upon) on waking. You'll likely be amazed at the messages that come through when you look back at them during the day.

Friendships

Coming out of Deep Shift, there will be no more pretending when it comes to friendships—these are either your people or they're not. Some friendships will naturally fall away, and that's all good. Other friendships are likely going to deepen, and these people will become your soul family. These are the ones to focus your time and energy on now, as these are the people who are going to be there for you, and who you will have no trouble leaning on when necessary. Now is the time to choose wisely and cherish those who make the cut. As for when people don't act how you would like them to, or you feel like you have been slighted by someone? Remember, it's not your job to judge. Just give it up to God and continue to stay in your lane. Say a short prayer for anyone who hurts you and just move on.

Find your people. If the above process finds you looking around wondering, "Where did everybody go?" remember: it's not them, it's you. You are a *new* you now, and so it's on you to actively seek out other like-minded souls. Sign up for group meditations, take classes you're interested in (especially spiritual classes), and put some effort into thinking about where you're likely to meet fellow Shifter souls. Putting in the work to find your people will soon find you cultivating new friendships that will last a lifetime.

Invest in your new friendships. You can feel a great connection from the get-go, but lasting friendships don't just happen. Social media has made us kinda lazy when it comes to creating connections that stick, so now is the time to go old-school and stage a get-together at your home, meet a new friend for coffee or tea, or simply *pick up the phone* for a conversation with a new pal. And remember: respect others' space and boundaries, always.

Stay open and vulnerable. Now is also the time to be open to meeting all sorts of folks. Because what you're going to be looking for in your friendships will likely be different—in fact, you can create a list similar to the one you made for your ideal romantic partnerships. What is a "good friend" to you? What will you no longer put up with? It's also very likely that you'll no longer have time for surface connections that don't really touch on what's happening below the surface. When it comes to keeping it *deep*, being vulnerable and real about what's up for you will give others permission to be the same with you.

Family

Here's the deal: there is a good chance your family members aren't going to get all this Shifter business, and that's okay. It isn't your job to make them understand, and it's *especially* not your job to force your ideas and experiences down their throats. This Shifter life is yours to just *be*. All you can do is love them the best you can and have a plan in place for if you find yourself in an uncomfortable position. Families can be challenging, especially for us Deep Shifters: in fact, it can even feel like our soul chose our family of origin for us in order for us to experience the very challenges that may have propelled us into Deep Shift. It's all good.

Stay in your lane. Keep your side of the street clean and try not to take shit personally. It may well be that you've been on a fast track to higher states of consciousness for many lifetimes, while your Aunt Barb is on her first go-around, and that her . . . shall we say . . . basic ideas about life reflect this. So be it. Don't let other family members' insistence that "this is the way we do things around here" drag you down. Just go with the flow and do the best you can to stay tuned in to your inner voice. Respond, don't react, and just keep calmly doing you.

And also get help as needed. If you have a particularly abusive or toxic family (emotional abuse totally counts here too), think about distancing yourself from them. For a while at least. If it comes to this, I also suggest getting professional help from a therapist. Disowning your family isn't easy, and it typically comes with lots of unwinding of childhood trauma (which we sometimes don't even see as such until after the lights go on during Deep Shift). This is not the kind of stuff you can—or should—be doing alone. Now is the time to bring out the big guns in terms of getting the support you need.

Let them do them. See everyone for who they are and, more importantly, *from where they are*. We don't all have to be the same, and we never *will* be. My mom often told me to look for one wonderful thing in each person I met and focus on that. This is *not* the same as ignoring any bad behavior and giving them a free pass to your inner world. It simply means choosing to pay attention to whatever positive attributes they do have and pouring your energy into that thing about them. This will help you see the whole person and have compassion for why they sometimes act the way they do.

Daily Routine

Finding your new daily routine is going to be the backbone of your full-powered Shifter existence. It sounds so mundane, but it really is what will keep the juju of the Universe/God flowing through you. Even more than the big, mind-and-spirit-expanding experiences that blow your soul wide open, what you do on the daily is actually what is going to keep you strong, clear, and on an even keel. Why? It all comes back to energy. When you've been through Deep Shift, even the smallest energy leaks can leave you feeling burned out and off-key, and when these build up over time you're on a fast track to nowhere good. A solid daily routine will keep your energy close and in check, the better to be channeled into what, and who, you are truly here to experience in this life.

Prioritize what feels good. Make a list of all the things that make you feel *wonderful*. Do you love to take a long walk after dinner in the evening? Does getting up an hour early to give you time to fully "arrive" in your waking life set you up for a stress-free day? Is having a daily debriefing with your bestie a must? Think of all the things that feed your soul and pick three or four that can become part of your schedule *every single day*. No excuses. No skipping.

Don't overthink it. Your daily routine should fit you like a glove, and if you find yourself putting too much effort into it you're likely veering off the path. Effort that doesn't feel *satisfying* is another energy leak! Adding some yoga, meditation, or a nature walk in the morning may seem like a great idea, but it might be that these things actually leave you feeling drained. On the other hand, something that at first feels awkward or challenging to add to your schedule may quickly begin to feel like a no-brainer—with the no-brainer being what we're aiming for here (thinking = overrated). When trying something new, give it a week or two to see how it sits and if it's a fit. Experiment with adding different things at different times of the day. And if it's just not working, drop it and move on.

Expect life to get easier. Having a good daily routine should feel like it's simplifying your life. As if you are checking the engine every day and making the wheels of your existence run smoother. Keep asking yourself: is this adding to, or detracting from, my energy? The key is to create a routine that works for you, that takes little to no effort to maintain, and that keeps you humming like a bird.

Spiritual Practice

Learn it. Live it. Love it. Even if you didn't have a dedicated spiritual practice before Deep Shift, it's likely you now have a whole new appreciation for the concept of a Higher Power—and you'll want to ensure you are staying connected to this aspect of your life through regular practice. Finding the spiritual practice that's right for you is going to be the juice that keeps your Shifter soul in a state of higher consciousness. This may be one of the most important parts of this puzzle. DO NOT BLOW IT OFF.

Find your spirituality. Depending on the kind of upbringing you had, chances are you have some preconceived ideas about spirituality—and you may have even decided that "religion" is not for you. But now is the time to question *everything you think you know* in this area (because, remember, chances are it's wrong!) and discover which spiritual practice *keeps* the magic flowing in your world. For me, nothing can even come close to a daily meditation practice. But maybe for you it's yoga, prayer or chanting, astrology, or the Tarot. Whatever your thang is, go for it and find a way to incorporate it into your daily routine.

Find your teachers. Follow your inner knowing to the ones who really *get it*. When you find them, read their books, take their courses, and seek to align their knowledge and wisdom with your own experience of life. The reason for working with a spiritual teacher is to understand *why* you are doing what you are doing and *why* you are having the experiences you are having. However, be wary of any self-proclaimed gurus who claim to have all the answers: the best teachers will help you find the answers that already lie within you.

But don't overdo it. Staying regular with your meditation practice, chanting, yoga class, or whatever path you have chosen to follow is going to be the backbone for this whole party. It's what will keep you connected to your higher self, the Universe, all the good juju, and the big magic. But don't go overboard. The goal is to marry your spiritual side with your regular human life. Going too far one way or the other will find you out of balance—and maybe even back where you started!

So there we have it. Follow the basics of my Real-World Maintenance Plan, and you'll be feeling more like yourself (but your shiny, new, super-charged self) in no time. But the real key to making the most of this one wild and precious Shifter life? Have a blast. Every. Damn. Day. Have fun, don't take things too seriously, and laugh as often as you can! Surround yourself with people you adore. Seek out magical experiences. And above all, *go for it*. Meaning, go all in, in your life, with your relationship with God, and in everything you do. With this recipe, you cannot lose. If doubts begin to get the best of you, step back, use your tools, and remind yourself: everything happens on God's time. We Shifters are a people of faith. We know the Universe has our back. We are not prisoners of time. And we know that we are being taken care of. Always.

CHAPTER 11

Transformed People
Transform People

"God grant to me that I may see . . .
the way to lift a brother up."

Unknown

Whenever I meet anybody who has made it through Deep Shift, I want to congratulate them. I'm so proud of them, I could cry. Because not only have they transformed themselves, but they are also in the process of transforming their little corner of the world and will continue to do so. Anybody who walks this path is gifted a quiet yet profound achievement: the awakening of their true self, which is a light whose rays will continue illuminating all they touch for as long as they're alive, and beyond.

My mother may have shared with me that Mother Teresa singlehandedly changed the world, but the saintly woman herself famously once said: "I alone cannot change the world, but I can cast a stone across the waters to create many ripples." Now, you are the stone that's going to bring wave after wave of change to the life of every person you encounter. I know, I know; you had no idea you were signing up for this. But while being in Deep Shift is an individual journey—it is *also* a reflection of a global shift in consciousness that's occurring.

And it all begins with you. Hear me loud and clear, my friend: going through Deep Shift means you have the magic, now. The juice of the Universe is running through your veins. And as you go out into the world, people will be transformed just by being in your presence. How? You are 100 percent emitting a different frequency now. What I mean is that in facing the waves of change and surrendering to your inner transit system, you have cranked up the level of POWER in your body to the point where everyone who comes into contact with you will be able to feel it. They will feel the peace that comes from learning to be with what is; the stillness that you cultivate when you stop resisting change and go with whatever is present; and the love and empathy you cannot help but develop for every being on the planet as a result of really going through the shift. And they won't be able to help being swept up in the never-ending sense of wonder that emanates from every "graduate" of Deep Shift.

Perhaps you've heard the saying "hurt people hurt people." Basically, when we're going around like the walking wounded because we haven't gotten real with ourselves and looked at our crap, we project all the unacknowledged pain on the inside onto everybody we come into contact with. Yeah, there's a LOT of that going on out there. What I'm describing here is basically the opposite. After we awaken, we're now like a walking light show—helping illuminate the world for others with our presence alone. How freaking cool is that?

Shifters are the change-makers. But we do so by transforming ourselves first and foremost, which means transforming the planet in the most fundamental way possible. We can focus on charities, helping individuals in need, and doing good works in the world. And let's definitely keep on doing all of this! But at the end of the day, the one thing that's really going to change the world is you transforming yourself. Why? Because once we're able to live our lives as who we truly are, and doing what we're truly here to do, we can't help but be of service to others. *Just by being us.*

Any Deep Shifter reading these words will have already started to see this happen—beginning with the simple fact that the choices you're making in the world are radically different than before. Now imagine what it would look like if a huge number, say *the majority of people all over the planet*, began making choices for themselves and their lives that came from this more conscious, less anxious, and more trusting place. Do you think we would see the same levels of violence, poverty, anxiety, and depression playing out in the world? Let me answer that question for you: *Hell to the no.* What we would see is a whole lot more generosity, acceptance, and peace.

Now let's take it a step further. What if the awakened, higher state of consciousness that has become your new normal was every single person's reality? What if it was channeled into our schools, our government, our food production, our health care? Can you imagine what a beautiful world we would have? It brings tears of joy to my eyes even thinking about it—especially considering how far we are from this vision currently.

What I'm describing here is a world where more of us have worked through all of our traumas—which is essentially what Deep Shift will do for a person. We can't fake being annihilated and coming back stronger than ever. And we can't fake being touched by the hand of God. It's black-and-white. You have either been through Deep Shift and come out the other side . . . or you haven't. When we find ourselves in this process, what we're being taught is how to respect our nervous-system responses ("triggers") and respond when necessary, versus reacting to every little thing.

There's never going to be a time when there isn't a boatload of issues in the world, but if you're good on the inside you'll have the resilience to ride the waves of change—and in doing so, show others how to do the same. Deep Shift gives you compassion for yourself first and foremost. Actually feeling our own pain is what helps us feel the pain of others. And once we get to this place, there's no more pretending that we aren't all here to help each other heal. This is the real gift of the Shift. You come out wanting to do good and help others because you GET IT.

I mean, while we're here imagining a whole new world, can you picture what this world would be like if everybody had been through the school of Deep Shift? It's hard to envision, because again it's *so* far from where we're at today. I will say, though, that the pleasures of the world—all the trinkets and prizes and accolades we get so caught up chasing, believing they are what will make us feel happy and whole—would seem completely boring and irrelevant.

Instead, we will aspire to create a softer world, and a more harmonious Universe. We may even find ourselves in a place where all people get to do what they love and are naturally good at every single day. It goes without saying that this world would champion equality and support for everyone. And that instead of trying to "one up" each other, we would do our best to appreciate and love each other. Finally, instead of enslaving and extracting from the animals, trees, and resources of the nonhuman world, we would instinctively protect and nurture the environment. I mean, all I'm talking about here is the original Golden Rule: treat others as you would like to be treated. For anybody who's made it through Deep Shift, who has seen the bottom of the bottom and had their world turned upside down and inside out, living this way *is as natural as breathing*.

The Path Forward

As for what comes next, I strongly suggest you take your newfound transformation and do some good works in the world with it. The Earth needs your wisdom, your love, and your beautiful, awakened soul like never before. How to begin? Follow where the Universe leads you. By the way, its "nudges" can come in all different forms. Sometimes they'll feel like quiet urges. An urge to pick up an instrument, an urge to write a play, an urge to call a friend you haven't spoken to in ages, an urge to do nothing and simply sit still and be quiet. These are all raindrops of information falling on you. Stick your tongue out, let them saturate you with inspiration, and then take it all in.

Your job is to just look out for the signs and follow them with your whole heart. I pinky-promise you those signals from the Universe will lead you to the Promised Land, or at least a life filled with unexpected adventures and fascinating experiences. You are now leading the life your Shifter soul has always deeply desired. You may of course feel called to help in some more obvious way, by becoming a social worker, a public speaker, a poet, or a CEO. Some of you may be drawn to parenthood. Others may feel inspired to go back to school or run for office. But it really doesn't matter what road you take: the common denominator is that whatever it is will feel like *your calling*. This may or may not be the thing you do to pay the rent; but it will, in some way, lead to you helping the world.

Because the fact is, we Deep Shifters naturally want to help guide and support people; we care for our fellow humans and feel inclined to build them up. It's just our nature. Why? Because going through Deep Shift gives us empathy for others' suffering. We can't help but see all the challenges they have been through because we've been there too—and THIS is what makes us potential world-changers. When we've been through it ourselves it becomes impossible to watch others suffering and not step in, right? Also, we now know—in a way nobody learns in school—how to deal when life gives you reallllly sour lemons . . . so we can become an example for others just by living as our Shifter selves!

The final great thing I want to share about making it through Deep Shift is this: you will recognize your fellow Shifters everywhere you go, and you will open your arms to them, like dear old friends. These people are your "brothers and sisters from another mother," and they are operating on the same Cosmic wavelength as you. Hold on to them, cherish them, and be grateful for their friendship. These people are beyond precious; they are your official Shifter tribe members.

And remember, there is power in numbers. When Shifters come together in one place to induce change, they will create a tipping point: as defined by Merriam-Webster, "the critical point in a situation, process, or system, beyond which a significant or even unstoppable effect or change takes place." All you Shifters, hear me now: *we are the future*. We are the change that has the power to change everything!

If I can leave you with anything more, it's that going through Deep Shift has gifted you with the ability to DO this thing called Life and do it brilliantly. Meaning, you choose to love your fellow humans, animals, and nature itself unconditionally. To be a beacon of peace and love, so that your people can find you. To give everyone you meet permission to let go too, and to play and flourish. To allow yourself to be happy and to let joy wash over you. To plow ahead when the going gets tough, knowing that you are under God's protection, every step of the way. And above all, to know that you too, no matter what, are deeply, deeply loved.

Acknowledgments

First and foremost, I want to thank my incredible agent, Coleen O'Shea, for pushing me to be the best possible version of myself. I am forever grateful for your guiding hand.

To my editors, Willy Mathes and Ruby Warrington, your patience, brilliance, and kindness has been a gift. This book would not be possible without you.

To all my friends and family, thank you for always supporting my dreams. I love you.

Lastly, to my publisher, Sounds True, and specifically Diana Ventimiglia, I am honored to work side by side with you.

Thank you for everything,

Valerie C. Gangas

Notes

Chapter 5: Fill Up at the Meditation Station

Thich Nhat Hanh, "The Sutra on Knowing the Better Way to Live Alone," abuddhistlibrary.com/Buddhism/G - TNH/TNH/The Sutra On Knowing The Better Way to Live Alone/The Sutra on Knowing the Better Way to Live Alone.htm

UKEssays, "Sleep Is a Facilitator of Information Processing," ukessays.com/essays/psychology/sleep-is-a-facilitator-of-information-processing-psychology-essay.php.

Chapter 6: Life Is Not an Out-of-Body Experience

Harvard Health, "Nutritional Strategies to Ease Anxiety," health.harvard.edu/blog/nutritional-strategies-to-ease-anxiety-201604139441

Dr. Axe, "Nitric Oxide Benefits and How to Increase Levels Naturally," draxe.com/nutrition/nitric-oxide-benefits/.

Annie's Apothecary, "Nitric Oxide and Mental Health," https://anniesrx.com/articles/nitric-oxide-and-mental-health.

Chapter 9: Welcome to the Other Side

Deepak Chopra, "Witnessing Sleep," deepakchopra.com/articles/witnessing-sleep/.

Anmol Mehta, "Psychic Powers - How You Can Get the Siddhis Safely," anmolmehta.com/psychic-powers-how-you-can-get-the-siddhis-safely/.

About the Author

Valerie Gangas has often been called "a force of nature"—she is *also* a transformational life coach, speaker, and author of the Amazon bestseller *Enlightenment Is Sexy: Every Woman's Guide to a Magical Life*. After her first Transcendental Meditation experience in the winter of 2011, Valerie's spiritual awakening inspired a nonstop outpouring of creativity, insight, and empowerment; thus *Enlightenment Is Sexy* was born.

Standing firmly in her belief that "life is best lived from the inside out," Valerie uses her coaching, speaking, writing—including this, her latest book, *In Deep Shift*—and expanding social media platforms to share her illuminating discoveries so others may find the inspiration, encouragement, and guidance, especially when life seems most challenging and bewildering, to reclaim their lives, transform their consciousness, and make their dreams of happiness, peace, and abundance come true.

"Consciousness, freedom, purpose, and love are what it's all about," she says, and this provocative 21st-century mantra is the focus of Valerie's multi-dimensional approach to helping people in the midst of radical change find a new, profoundly awakened perspective and the best of it all in their daily lives. For more, visit valeriegangas.com.